BRICK TOWER PRESS   GARDEN GUIDE

Flowerbeds and Borders
in
Deer Country

for the Home and Garden

A BRICK TOWER PRESS GARDEN GUIDE

Flowerbeds and Borders
in
Deer Country

by Vincent Drzewucki Jr.

Interior Illustrations   *Cover Illustration*
Alison Gail   Lisa Adams

The Brick Tower Press ®
1230 Park Avenue, New York, NY 10128
Text Copyright © 2005
by Vincent Drzewucki Jr.
Interior Illustrations Copyright © 2005 by Brick Tower Press

Drzewucki Jr., Vincent
A Brick Tower Press Garden Guide

Includes Index
ISBN 1-883283-29-9 softcover

Library of Congress Control
Number: 2005925354
First Printing, June 2005

CONTENTS

GROUND-COVERS

VINES

PERENNIALS

ANNUALS

BULBS

HERBS

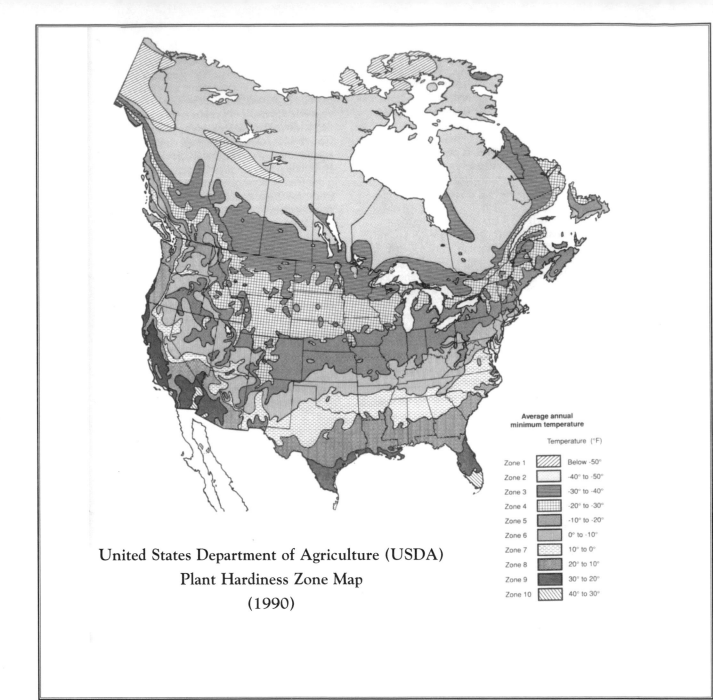

Average annual minimum temperature

Temperature (°F)

Zone 1		Below -50°
Zone 2		-40° to -50°
Zone 3		-30° to -40°
Zone 4		-20° to -30°
Zone 5		-10° to -20°
Zone 6		0° to -10°
Zone 7		10° to 0°
Zone 8		20° to 10°
Zone 9		30° to 20°
Zone 10		40° to 30°

United States Department of Agriculture (USDA)

Plant Hardiness Zone Map

(1990)

INTRODUCTION

More and more, homeowners and gardeners throughout rural and suburban America have been forced to deal with a growing menace....

Deer!

From coast to coast, deer have developed quite an appetite for almost anything growing in our landscapes and gardens.

Deer frequently feed on flowers, fruits, vegetables and the twigs of trees and shrubs, often permanently disfiguring them. In winter, bucks rub their antlers on sapling trees and shrubs, severely damaging the bark and seriously threatening the health and life of the plant. As a result, deer have become a big a nuisance to home gardeners and professionals who design and maintain landscapes and gardens.

The economic costs caused by deer browsing damage in the U.S. amounts to millions of dollars every year. Replacing plantings is one thing but even more is spent on repellents, fences and numerous other strategies for protecting landscapes, home gardens and agricultural crops from deer browsing damage.

Suburban sprawl, increased abandoned farmlands and unchecked growing populations of deer are just some of the reasons deer have become such a costly nuisance around the country.

> "Abundant Whitetails Munch Through the Underbrush; 'Like the Serengeti Plain'"
>
> – James P. Sterba,
> *The Wall Street Journal*

WHAT THIS BOOK IS ABOUT

The purpose of this book is to help and guide home gardeners and professionals with creating pleasing and colorful flowerbeds and borders in deer country by using deer resistant flowers and other plants.

With a list of well over 350 flowers and ornamental plants, *Flower Beds and Borders in Deer Country* will help you select plants that are known to have a resistancy to deer browsing damage. By making the right choices you'll be able to significantly reduce or eventually eliminate the need for using repellents, fences and other means of protecting your garden from damage by deer.

Flowerbeds and Borders in Deer Country focuses on herbaceous flowering plants, ornamental soft- stemmed flowering plants and plants valued for their interesting foliage. All plants listed are known to be resistant to browsing. Included are lists of annual and perennial flowering plants, groundcovers, vines, flower bulbs, herbs and ornamental grasses that are known to have a resistancy to deer browsing damage in most areas of the continental U.S.

The idea for this book is sort of an offshoot of my first book, *Gardening in Deer Country*, which was first published in 1998.

A surprising success, *Gardening in Deer Country* is an attempt to help home gardeners and professionals alike, from coast to coast, select plants such as trees, shrubs, perennials, annuals, bulbs, groundcovers, vines and herbs that are known to have a resistance to browsing deer for use in land-scapes and gardens. Over the years, as I've heard from individuals throughout the US and Canada, amateurs and professionals alike who have had success using the plants suggested in *Gardening in Deer Country* the plants listed are useful coast to coast where deer browsing is a problem.

Flowerbeds and Borders in Deer Country focuses on colorful flowers and ornamental plants that are best suited for flowerbeds and borders and features a new expanded list of over 250 herbaceous plants and advice for how to design flowerbeds and borders. All of the plants listed in both books are hardy down to an average minimum temperature of 10 to 0 degrees F. or zone 7 of the USDA Plant hardiness Zone Map (1990) although many are hardy down to zone 2 (-40 to -50 F) and many will do well in zone 8 (20 to 10 F).

Ageratum or Flossflower, *Ageratum houstonianum,* **page 77**

The Fun Part of Gardening

Recently, the use of herbaceous flowering plants, that is - annual bedding plants, perennial flowers, herbs and bulbs (perennials are the ones that return year after year), has become very popular in home landscapes and gardens. While trees and shrubs provide a long term, somewhat permanent framework in the home landscape, flowerbeds and borders add color and interest and are flexible and easy to change, season-to-season or year-to-year.

For many, planting and maintaining annual and perennial flowers is the real fun part of gardening. Flowerbeds and borders are different things to different gardeners. They can consist of all annuals, all perennials, or a combination of both and often include flowering trees and shrubs, both evergreen and deciduous and ornamental grasses.

Most home landscapes and gardens are a little bit of everything. Flowering plants are perhaps the most interesting and diverse group of plants to work with and the most fun, although a good garden or landscape design does include trees and shrubs as the framework. Flowering plants are very flexible in the landscape and garden, if you want to change a color scheme, a look, a theme, or include this year's hot new introductions, no problem. With a minimal amount of work it can be attained.

New annuals are planted each spring anyway and perennials, although considered somewhat more permanent in the garden since they come back year after year, even they can be easily moved and shifted around to create a new look.

A Word About Herbs

Don't forget to include herbs when gardening in deer country. Besides their culinary, cosmetic, medicinal and other uses, many herbs look great, are often very deer resistant and their delightful fragrances and scents often repel deer too! Herbs can be used in combination with many plants and should be included in any good deer resistant garden design. Most herbs have great ornamental value in the landscape and garden.

Each year there are many new introductions of exciting new varieties of old favorites such as Basil, Lavender, Mint and Thyme that look, smell, and taste great to us, but not to deer. In fact, the aromatic scent of herbs and other strongly scented plants will often act to protect and fragrantly camou-

Thyme, *Thymus vulgaris*, page 75

flage lesser deer resistant plants, so you just might be able to have that favorite plant that's proven to be prone to deer browsing damage if it's surrounded by more aromatic herbs and other deer resistant plants.

Proper Selection Makes Good Sense

When first confronted with deer browsing damage, somehow the thought of constantly applying repellents or making huge investments in specialized fencing material doesn't seem to make sense, practically and economically. Although some are very effective, these solutions can be costly, are at times aesthetically displeasing and often require frequent and period application and maintenance, sometimes forever!

Deer browsing is a pest problem. Today, pest problems are dealt with in landscape and gardens much differently than they were a few years ago. Applying a "pesticide" on a regular basis used to be the most popular method of control. More recently however, concerns about pesticide use and its long and short-term effect on the health of humans and wildlife and the environment have become a great concern.

To reduce and eliminate the use of toxic pesticides, many home gardeners and professional have learned to use least-toxic alternative methods of pest control that include carefully selecting and planting only those plants or varieties that are resistant to certain pest problems and ones that are well-suited to site conditions. This often leads to the eventual removal or discarding of those plants that frequently succumb to insect and/or disease problems which act as a pest magnet. This system or process of using proper plant selection to control pest problems is part of a larger system of pest management strategies known as Integrated Pest Management or IPM for short. Selecting and using plants that are known to be resistant to deer browsing is considered an IPM strategy too.

Chapter 5 lists the more deer resistant plants to choose from.

IPM strategies also include determining a threshold of tolerance for an acceptable amount of damage by a pest problem. When damage levels exceed threshold levels, causing significant economic or unacceptable aesthetic plant damage, then the use of alternative methods of control such as the use of repellents, fences or the replacement of plants with plants that are resistant to deer browsing make sense.

Although many deer repellents are natural or contain organic ingredients, their initial cost and future costs for repeated application need to be carefully considered. Even a fence, with its initial costs for materials and installation, also has long-term maintenance costs associated with its use.

Certainly a small amount of deer browsing damage can be tolerated in a landscape or garden, but when deer eat the entire contents of the flowerbed or permanently disfigure a tree or shrub then some form of action is necessary.

How much damage is too much damage? It all depends on what you determine is acceptable. Control under IPM is accomplished by utilizing various types of control options based upon economic, ecological and sometime sociological factors. IPM is really a philosophy of how one controls pest problems. When all the potential possibilities for controlling deer browsing damage are weighed, it seems to me that selecting and planting those plants that deer just don't like to eat seems to make the most sense.

On average, a healthy adult buck needs to consume 5-10 pounds of food each day.

THE DEER FACTS

More and more, garden and landscape professionals as well as wildlife experts are asked what can be done to reduce and eliminate damage to ornamental plants in landscapes and gardens caused by deer. As the population shifts from congested suburban and urban areas to more rural areas, new home sites invade native deer habitats and as a result, deer browsing damage becomes ever more common.

The deer family in the US consists primarily of two species of deer, the white-tailed deer (Odocoileus virginianus) which inhabits most of the U.S. and the mule deer (Odocoileus hemionus) found primarily west of the Mississippi River. Numerous subspecies of both exist.

The primary distinguishing characteristic used for identifying the mule deer is its large ears and slightly larger size and weight. The deer family also includes caribou, elk and moose, however the white-tailed deer are considered to be the greatest nuisance to the home gardener.

Not only does the homeowner and gardener suffer from deer damage, commercial enterprises suffer as well. Commercial landscapes are prone to deer damage while it's estimated that hundreds of thousands of dollars are lost each year to deer browsing damage at nurseries producing trees, shrubs and other ornamental plants. Other agricultural crops, fruits and vegetables for example incur damage as well.

The purpose of this book, however, is to guide homeowners and professionals throughout the US and Canada in making the right choices of herbaceous plants or alternative defenses that will eliminate or reduce deer damage in and around their gardens and home property.

The return of the white-tail deer is by and large a paradoxical event. Their return, considered a miracle by some, is at the same time a growing cause of economic destruction. University studies by Cornell Cooperative Extension's and other institutions show that deer populations are growing. Once reduced to a population of not more than 500,000 deer in the US around 1900, estimates today are that the white-tailed deer numbers may now exceed 15 million.

Estimates show that in densely populated areas 90-100 deer per 100 acres are not uncommon. The white-tail deers' come back is attributed to several factors such as, restricted use of firearms and tougher hunting laws, diminished or nonexistent populations of natural predators such as wolves and bobcats, conversion of abandoned agricultural lands back into deer friendly habitats.

Deer do damage by browsing, a pattern of feeding in which they select tender shoots, twigs and leaves of plants and by rubbing their antlers on tree sapling and shrubs. Although deer are known to be finicky eaters, they are known to eat more than 500 different kinds of plants. Their taste can change and depends primarily on the season, nutritional needs and the abundance or lack of abundance of their favorite foods. Be assured however that if and when times are bad and preferred foods are scarce, deer will eat just about anything.

On average, a healthy adult buck (male), which stands about 3 - 4 feet tall and weighs anywhere from 125 to 200 pounds, does (females) are smaller,

needs to consume 5-10 pounds of food (4,000-6000 calories) per day. Although this may not sound like a lot, just think how many tender new shoots, twigs and leaves it would take to satisfy a deer daily, and since deer often browse in groups of 2-7, that's a lot of ornamental garden plants. New plantings and well fertilized and maintained gardens seem to be especially preferred by deer and since deer are creatures of habit, once a new feeding area is found to be to their liking, future damage is easily predictable.

Like other wild animals such as raccoons, squirrels, rabbits and opossum to name a few, deer have learned to coexist with us in our suburban and rural areas and deer have learned to adapt to the changes we have imparted to their environment. In fact, many deer have lost their fear of us or have adjusted their feeding schedule to avoid us and our dogs. Deer venture into our gardens at dawn or dusk for an undisturbed, leisurely meal. The follow-

Snapdragon, *Antirrhinum majus*, page 77

ing section describes things we can do to prevent this from happening.

DEER DEFENSE

The primary purpose of this book is to help gardeners plan flowerbeds and borders that will be resistant to deer browsing. On the other hand, there may be situations where existing plantings may need protection from deer browsing damage.

Although many suggestions, solutions and products have existed in the field of horticulture for controlling deer browsing, it always seemed to me that the most logical and cost efficient way of preventing deer from making a meal of your garden was to plan it to be resistant by using plants that deer simply don't like to eat. In almost every situation deer tend to be very selective, making gluttons of themselves when they come across a favorite plant and more often than not, leaving less appealing plants alone. So, as a result, I've come up with an extensive list of plants in chapter 5 that are known to be least preferred by deer. Whether you're planning new flowerbeds and borders or just trying to renovate and convert an existing garden, the lists provided in chapter 5 will serve as guide for selecting the best plants for having a beautiful deer-proof garden in deer country.

Tried and True Methods of Deer Defense

Here are some alternative methods of deer defense strategies that have been used and are available to reduce deer damage in gardens and landscapes that currently exist.

There are several ways to protect a garden and the surrounding property from deer browsing damage. Some are long term while others are very temporary. Most commonly used methods are fencing, chemical or organic repellents, electronic sound devices, dogs, and of course, using deer resistant plants. Each has its own unique advantages and disadvantages. Each may be used by itself or in combination to attain an effective means of control.

FENCES

The fence provides perhaps the best means of protection against deer damage. A physical barrier, a fence is a somewhat permanent physical structure in the garden or landscape. To keep deer out it must be 8 feet or taller, anything lower may act as a deterrent for some time, however, deer can usually easily jump any fence less than 8 feet if they need to. Care must also be taken to sink the fencing mesh or woven wire into the ground 18-24 inches deep since deer have been known to crawl under loosely constructed fences.

For flowerbed and border protection, an 8 foot fence is, to say the least, ridiculous, being better suited for surrounding larger areas or the perimeter of a landscape. The initial cost, especially on a large piece of land plus the fact that a fence may need periodic maintenance or total replacement in 20-30 years make using a fence rather costly. Also, a fence is usually highly visible and can detract from the aesthetic beauty of the garden and property. However, in certain situations a fence may be an economical and ideal choice especially when used to enclose and protect let's say a vegetable garden, or a cut flower garden or other specialty plantings that need protection.

Electric fences also provide an effective alternative. They may not be as costly initially as other physical barrier fences, but they do require periodic maintenance, can be costly to operate over time, needing a constant power source and may need to be replaced more frequently.

Rather than going through the expense of building a substantial fence, a simple and less costly method may prove effective at keeping deer out. Install posts around the vegetable or flower garden and run a few lines of heavy gauge fishing line, 50 lbs. test or more. The deer run into the line, dislike it and go no further. This creates an almost invisible barrier and leaves the garden untouched by deer.

Oddly enough however, some gardeners have had success with using wire mesh, like chicken wire, or plastic netting, the kind used to protect fruit trees and berries from bird damage. The wire mesh or netting is laid horizontally on the ground surrounding the garden. It seems deer don't like the feel of walking on it and apparently don't like getting their legs tangled in it.

To protect individual plants or small plantings from deer browsing, especially in winter or early spring, a wire cage or plastic netting can be used. In winter, wrap the trunks of young trees and shrubs with wire mesh to protect trees from damage by bucks rubbing their antlers.

For more extensive and detailed information on constructing fences for protection from deer contact your local Cooperative Extension office.

REPELLENTS

By and large deer are creatures of habit. It has often been observed that a small herd of deer will walk past a perfectly good meal in someone's garden, or avoid a few rows of scrumptious potted plants in a nursery to browse elsewhere where they might feel safer or where they have been in the habit of browsing in the past. In part, repellents act to modify or control the behavior of deer, allowing them to habitually avoid certain areas while learning to find dependable browsing areas elsewhere.

Unfortunately, however, it's hard to tell how long a particular repellent will work or how long it will need to be used. Repellents may need to be periodically changed to avoid having deer getting used to any one particular product.

There are numerous repellents on the market that are effective. Most are organic chemicals that act as an odorous barrier while others repel by giving the plants they are sprayed on a disagreeable taste to the deer. There are even now electronic audio devices now available that repel by sound. All provide an invisible, although temporary or seasonal means of control. Most are effective when repeatedly applied every 2-4 weeks or according to label directions, while others must be applied after every rainfall or after using sprinklers.

Most repellents are based on odors or tastes that deer don't like. Deer find them either unpleasant or disturbing because they resemble the scent of a predator or danger while others make the plants they are applied on taste bad. Repellents are available commercially in Garden Centers, Hardware and Farm Stores and through mail order and online catalogs. These products are often formulations of ammonium soaps and non-commercial ingredients such as deodorant soaps, human hair, coyote and bobcat urine, or tankage (agricultural by-products such as dried manure, blood and other animal residues). Some of the most effective repellents contain garlic or putrescent egg solids, which provides a "rotting egg" odor, while ingredients such as capsaicin (hot pepper) or thiram, (a mild fungicide), make plants taste bad.

When buying and using commercial repellents, always read and follow the label directions and make sure they are labeled for use on the plants you are trying to protect and be especially cautious around vegetables, fruits and berries. Some repellents may have a toxic effect on the plant it's applied to. If you're not sure call the manufacturer or try it on a small section of the plant on an inconspicuous location on the plant. If it's not compatible a bad reaction will show up within a day or two.

Repellents can be costly and time consuming to apply and often must be re-applied after rain. How long they will remain effective and need to be applied is uncertain. Certain repellents depend on certain temperature ranges to be effective and the choice of repellent may change seasonally. Some may lose their potency soon after being applied during the spring due to expanding new vigorous growth.

The effectiveness of repellents will depend primarily on weather, the growth rate of the plants being protected, the current availability of natural food sources, a deer's appetite, stage of development, and frequency of application.

Commercial deer repellents can be found under these and numerous other name brands: BOBBEX, Bye Deer- All Natural Deer Repellent, Deer-Away Big Game Repellent, Liquid Fence Deer Repellent, Hinder Deer and Rabbit Repellent, Repellex, Scoot Deer, Sudbury Detour Rabbit and Deer Repellent Tree Guard Deer Repellent, and TreeWorld Plantskydd Deer Repellent.

This list does not imply an endorsement of these products, however these and many other deer repellent products on the market have been found to provide good protection from deer browsing damage. Result may vary from location to location and season to season. For numerous reasons, products may loose their effectiveness over time and alternative products may need to be tried as a replacement.

HOME REMEDIES

Milorganite is one of the most effective organic deer repellents. The regular use of Milorganite on lawn areas and around flowers, trees, and shrubs in the garden and in containers and pots provides proven results. The benefits are twofold.

Milorganite is one of the best organic lawn and garden fertilizers around, it's non-burning and is a 100% natural organic fertilizer. Its main purpose is for fertilizing lawns, trees, shrubs, flowers and vegetables, keeping plants healthy and vigorous.

Milorganite is also an excellent deer repellent when used around plants to be protected. Apply at a rate of 5 pounds per 100 square feet as frequently as every 2 weeks. It's an all natural and organic fertilizer that's made from activated sewage sludge from the Milwaukee Sewage District in Wisconsin. Documented studies conducted by Cornell Cooperative Extension in Dutchess County, New York have found Milorganite to be a very effective deer repellent.

Dried Blood Meal is a form of tankage (an agricultural by-product) and offers protection from deer damage. Like Milorganite, dried blood meal is good for plants as a natural organic fertilizer, a good source of nitrogen for plants. Nitrogen promotes green growth in plants.

For best results, Dried Blood Meal should be mixed with water and sprayed on plants. Scattering Dried Blood Meal in its dry form around the base of plants is second best, be sure to lightly wet it to activate its odorous affect. To prevent deer damage Dried Blood Meal must be applied on a weekly basis and following heavy rains.

Bars of Deodorant Soap hung on or near susceptible plants is effective within a range of three to four feet. Soap bars can be left in their original wrappers and hung with string or wire. Insert the string or wire through a hole, drilled into the bar's center. Or, make small pouches by cutting up old sheets, stockings, panty hose or mesh onion bags into 8 inch squares. Cut soap bars in half and place half a soap bar in middle of square. Gather corners and tie up with string or rubber bands. As the bars work best when kept wet, leave the wrappers on to make them work better and last longer. Most deodorant soaps work well, but experiment with different brands. Lifebuoy brand

consistently produces the best result. Replace as needed.

Human Hair is an effective odorous repellent. You can collect human hair from barbershops (hair from beauty salons may not be as effective). Put a few handfuls of hair in the small pouches made as described above and place throughout the garden 3-4 feet apart hanging on branches or stakes. Replace hair in pouches midway through the growing season to prolong effectiveness.

HOMEMADE RECIPES

For an effective deer repellent spray use the following formula as a homemade deer repellent spray: 6 spoiled eggs, 3 tablespoons of Thiram 75% (a mild fungicide), 5 oz. of Tabasco or any other hot pepper sauce and 1 qt. Water. Mix thoroughly together, use an old blender if possible. (do not re-use blender canister for anything used for human or animal consumption). Then, add mixture to 3 gallons of water, mix thoroughly. Repeat as needed especially after rain or snow.

Small pouches for hanging on plants can be made by combining a cup of dried blood meal and a cup of human hair. Cut out 4 inch squares from old sheets, stockings, pantyhose and place a tablespoon or two of the mixture in the center of the square. Gather corners and tie up with string or wire and hang on plants to be protected.

Experiment on your own. What works in one area might not work so well in another. Try different combinations, varying the type and amount of ingredients until you find a recipe that works best for you.

SCARE AND SOUND DEVICES

There are numerous scare and sound making devices available for chasing deer out of landscapes and gardens. These include devices connected to a motion detector that use loud sounds such as whistles, sirens, gun shot (blanks), rock and heavy metal music, to frighten deer away.

Other devices include, motion detector triggered flashing bright lights, sprinklers and animated scarecrows. Recently, several companies have brought out on the market electronic ultrasound repellent equipment that repel deer and other animals by using sounds that can't be heard by humans, having a repelling affect in a very specific area and may not be practical. Depending on the landscape or garden design involved, the abundance and placement of plants and structures tend to block most of these units' effectiveness creating gaps where deer and other animals may feed unaffected. To achieve adequate protection in outdoor areas, several units may need to be employed at a cost of $80 or more per unit plus maintenance costs.

By and large however, most of these scare devices may become ineffective after a few days as deer begin to lose fear of these scare tactics. Also, the use of certain scare and sound device may violate local ordinances.

DOGS

A good size dog of the proper temperament will provide a simple and effective means of eliminating deer damage. The dog may be kept on a leash outdoors at night or may be free to roam within a fenced in area. A combination of a dog and the use of a 5-7 foot fence certainly will be an extremely effective control. The use of this dog/fence combination may prove to be much more affordable, practical and more aesthetically pleasing than the the costs and looks of an 8 foot high or taller deer-proof fence, although maintenance and replacement costs for both dog and fence may need to be considered too.

DESIGNING FLOWERBEDS
AND BORDERS

At first, deer in the garden may be a delightful and welcome sight. How could anyone ever want to harm or chase away these delightfully beautiful creatures? Some folks even go out of their way to provide them with a quick meal or salt lick. But if your passion is gardening, beware! These innocent, wide-eyed, furry visitors could quickly become the number one bane of your garden, eating all of your precious flowers and trampling down whatever they didn't eat. Luckily however there's such a vast array of colorful deer resistant flowering plants to choose from that it would difficult for any gardener to ever become bored of using and enjoying them. Yes, you can indeed have a beautiful garden in deer country.

Whether you are a beginning gardener or seasoned enthusiast, one of the best things about working with herbaceous flowers is that you can suit them to your experience, needs and budget. You can start small and simple, add and expand later on or if you already have flower gardens you can renovate and add to what's there already, keep it simple with a few mass plantings or

maybe even eventually convert your whole lawn into an English-style border or cottage garden with dozens of varieties of gorgeous flowers and herbs.

**Crainsbill, *Geranium*
page 68**

Before we go further, let's define some of the terms in this book that we'll be using:

HERBACEOUS is a word used to describe a soft-stemmed plant having no woody tissue above ground and usually persisting for a single growing season. Most of the plants in this book are herbaceous unless stated otherwise.

HARDY is a term used to describe a plant's ability to survive winter conditions without any protection. See USDA Plant Hardiness Zone Map.

ANNUALS are plants that grow and complete their life cycle within one year. They are not hardy in zones where the average annual minimum temperature may drop below freezing. Examples include: Ageratum, Impatiens, Marigolds and Petunias.

BIENNIALS generally these are plants that complete their life cycle in two years, putting forth blooms and setting seed in the second year. Sometimes it takes three years. Examples include: Forget-Me-Not and foxglove.

**Crown Imperial, *Fritillaria*,
page 83**

PERENNIALS are hardy plants (of varying degrees, see USDA Plant Hardiness Zone Map) that usually live for several years or more, though some are longer-lived than others depending on soil, climate insects, diseases and numerous other factors. Examples include: Beebalm, Black-Eyed-Susans, Coreopsis and Purple Coneflower.

BULBS a term used to describe plants that form an underground structure in the from of a modified bud (true bulbs), stem or root for storing food in the form of starches and sugars (carbohydrates) for future use usually after winter for putting forth flowers and new growth in spring.

**Black-Eyed-Susan, *Rudbeckia maxima*,
page 73**

There are hardy and non-hardy bulbs. Examples of hardy bulbs include: Daffodils, Hyacinths and Tulips.

HERBS are plants that are traditionally used for medicinal, culinary, cosmetic or utilitarian use. Many herbs have great orna-

**Basil, *Ocimum basilicum,*
page 90**

mental value in the garden and are often resistant to deer browsing. Examples include: Basil, Lavender and Thyme.

**Bugleweed, *Ajuga reptans,*
page 54**

GROUNDCOVERS are low growing plants that spread and form dense ground covering masses. May have woody or herbaceous stems. Examples include: Lady's Mantle, Ajuga, and Pachysandra.

ORNAMENTAL GRASSES are non-turf type grasses used in landscapes and gardens for their ornamental value. They may be annual or perennial. Examples include: Sedges, Switch grass, Zebra grass and Fountain grass.

BED a flat or level plot of ground where plants are grown.

BORDER a narrow bed of planted ground along the edge of a shrub planting, garden, patio, deck or walk.

A Word About Perennials

A common misconception about perennials is that once planted they are carefree. Occasionally this might be true, but for the most part, perennials and most hardy plants will need a little help getting established and for keeping them healthy and vigorous over the years. Watering, weeding, pruning and deadheading, digging and dividing, fertilizing, controlling pest problems and staking are some of the chores needed for maintaining great looking perennials in flowerbeds and borders.

Annuals bedding plants, biennials and most other herbaceous plants will also require similar care.

Start With a Plan

Before buying or planting it's always a good idea to have a plan for your garden. Start by drawing an overhead view plan of the planting area. For most home projects a rough sketch is all you will need. Begin with paper and a pencil and a good eraser. Draw the existing area including buildings and other permanent structures such as walks/paths. fences, driveways, etc and existing trees and shrubs. Then using the pencil and eraser draw in flowerbed shapes or boundaries. Within the flowerbed areas draw in areas indicating groupings for the various varieties of plants. Write in the names of the plants within the various areas.

Shapes and names can be changed, added or taken out using the pencil and eraser. The use of overlays drawn on tranparent or tracing paper will allow you to create several designs, enabling you to

choose the best one. Just draw what exists first, then overlay the transparent or tracing paper and draw in the new design.

Keep relative size relationships as accurate as possible. Using a ruler or scale will help with size relationships. Perhaps 1 inch on your paper could be equal to 12 inches or one foot of actual area. Better yet, use graph paper instead and let each square be equal to12 inches or one foot.

Experiment on paper, developing several alternatives. It is much easier to change a design or placement of plants or groupings or structures on paper with an eraser than it is to change that same design in the actual landscape or garden with a shovel.

For big projects it pays to hire a pro-

fessional designer to work with, their knowledge and experience will be worth every penny in the long run. A good designer wil analyze the site and create a design that will work best, taking into consideration all factors like existing sunlight exposures, soils, drainage, existing structures, and peoper selection.

Be Creative

There are many ways to grow and enjoy flowers. Herbaceous flowering plants come in many sizes, colors, shapes, textures and bloom times. Combinations are limitless, from impressive grand scale 20 x 200 foot long English-style borders, with their lavish use of bold colors, heights and textures to a simple potted plant in a stylish container strategically placed on a patio, deck or doorstep.

Many of us don't have the luxury of being able to create the classic borders commonly found on estates, parks and botanical gardens, however beautiful flowerbeds and borders can be incorporated into almost any size landscape.

Beds and borders are traditionally located in full sun, however even an area shaded by deciduous trees can become a spot for a woodland garden by incorporating deer resistant and shade tolerant shrubs with beds and borders full of spring flowering bulbs and shade tolerant annuals and perennials. Even simple mass plantings of large swaths of colorful annuals or perennials around or among trees and shrubs in home landscapes can provide a creative and bold new look to a landscape.
For most of us an integrated approach works best, one that mixes things up a bit.
Creating mixed flower beds and borders using annuals, biennials, perennials, bulbs, herbs, groundcovers and ornamental grasses around trees and shrubs, the real framework of most residential landscapes.

Sweet William, *Dianthus*, page 20, 41

Make Selections Wisely

No matter what your garden situation is, there are numerous deer resistant plants to choose from that will adapt to the conditions you already have. When making your selections it is important to know what the site conditions are to match the preferences of the plant with existing conditions. Ignoring plant preferences can put plants at risk and is often the primary reason for failure.

Observe and note the site conditions for the garden bed or border you're planning to plant. Is the area sunny or shady? Is the soil wet or dry? Clay? Sand? Check your soil's pH to determine how acidic or alkaline it is. Is the area very windy or somewhat protected? Make plant selections based on existing sunlight, soil and other existing factors or change them accordingly. How cold is your climate? When selecting perennials and other cold hardy plants make sure they are hardy in your area or zone (see USDA Hardiness Zone map) if you're expecting them to come back next year. And make note of when the last frost date is in your area for safely planting out tender annual seedlings and transplants.

Plan For Continuous Color

For continuous color some planning is required. Although most annual flowering plants will provide continuous blooms from spring when first planted until the first fall frost, most perennials, bulbs and other herbaceous flowering plants will not. Although there are some very long blooming perennials like Coreopsis, Purple Coneflower and Black-Eyed-Susan, most perennials bloom for only a few weeks and at different times. Some bloom, in spring while others in summer or fall. For constant color, select and plants groups of perennial plants that are long season bloomers and others that bloom spring, summer and fall.

Grouping Plants and Making Combinations Work

Although there are no set rules, there are some things to consider when planning your plantings. Be creative and go with your instincts. In most situations using a mass planting of a single color or type of plant works best. Large swaths of color provide the best impact. This usually works best for large areas and for landscapes that will be viewed from a distance or a busy street.

Use large plantings of a single color or type of plant to lead the eye or as a focal point, around or leading up to an entrance-way, garden ornament or other structure.

Mass plantings create a bold look and often makes for easier mainte-nance. For other situations, try creating attractive combinations by grouping plants that compli-ment each other with their color, shape and/or texture. Keep groupings simple. Generally, use three to five different types of plants to a group. Plant in masses to cre-ate large splashes of color and for greatest impact, especially in large gardens. A limited selec-tion of colors and textures will be more pleasant than the busy look of a multitude of colors. Planting at least three or more (any odd number will do) individual plants in a cluster will provide the best impact. The larger the area the greater the number of plants will be needed to create large splashes of color.

Anise, *Pimpinalla anisum,* page 91

Use repitition to tie different areas of the garden together and to create harmony. For the best effect, repeat the use of the same plant or flower color in several places throughout the flowerbed, border and gar-den. Mixing and matching colors, shapes and textures is like painting with flowers. This makes designing gar-den beds and borders or land-scapes fun. Make the most of the wide variety of plant material listed in chapter 5. Use the fol-lowing advice and tips to cre-ate your own beautiful garden in deer country.

COLOR

When it comes to annual and perennial flowers, even shrubs, you can find them in nearly every color of the rainbow. Color can set the mood and feel of a garden. The right selection and placement of color can make a garden come alive or can create a relaxing and calming retreat. Red and orange ranges are warm and welcoming, blues and violets have a cooler effect while shades of green and yellow are soothing and calming. Most of us have a favorite color or color scheme, a combination of colors from a favorite sweater or blouse, draperies or upholstery. Keep these favorite colors and combinations in mind when designing your garden or see how a new combination works.

THE COLOR WHEEL

Combining colors is easy using the color wheel. The color wheel is divided into three categories: primary, secondary, and tertiary. The three primary colors are red, yellow and blue. These colors are considered to be foundation colors because they are used to create all other colors. By combining two of the primary colors, three secondary colors are formed. They are orange, green and violet. The six tertiary colors are made by combining a primary and an adjacent secondary color. These colors are red-orange, red-violet, yellow-green, yellow-orange, blue-green and blue-violet.

Red   Orange

Violet   Yellow

Blue   Green

USE SHADES OF A SINGLE COLOR

Monochromatic color schemes work well especially when mixing flowers of different sizes and shapes and by choosing foliage with interesting textures and colors. By staying within one basic color group everything automatically pulls together.

Take shades of purple for instance, you can mix lavender, violet, and mauve flowers with purple foliage to your heart's content and have a great looking combination.

COMPLIMENTARY COLORS

Combine colors that are opposite each other on the color wheel as complementary partners - red and green, orange and blue, yellow and violet, etc. When used together they intensify each other and really make your displays stand out.

HARMONIOUS COLORS

These are colors that are next to each other on the color wheel, for example; blue and violet, red and orange, orange and yellow. Combining these colors creates a soothing and gentle feel. Harmonious color schemes unify the design while providing interest.

PASTELS

Create a tranquil mood using lavender, peach, soft pink and powder blue. Pastels work best when viewed up close, especially in small space gardens and tend to look washed out when used in mass or in full sun.

BRIGHT COLORS

Bold bright reds, sunny yellows and vibrant oranges will call attention to the eye, even at a distance. Using bright colors brings an energy and vibrancy to a garden design. Using bright colors really livens up a garden and draws attention.

COLOR ECHOES

This really pulls the garden design into harmony with surrounding structures and garden features. Choose a focal point plant, structure or garden ornament and build on its color or colors. Perhaps the color of the house or parts of the house, like the color of the front door, shutters or house trim. Repeat these colors in the garden with flowers or foliage of the same or use shades of that single color as suggested above. Or, have your house or trim paint custom blended to match the color of your favorite flower.

USE WHITE FOR ACCENT OR BRIGHTNESS

White goes with everything. Use white flowers to separate colors, accent mass plantings or brighten dark or shady garden areas or entranceways.

A word of caution about using too many colors and types of plants. Good garden design is not complicated, in fact simple is often better. Avoid using too many colors and different types of plants. Large masses of flowers of a few colors or varieties, repeated throughout the garden will have a more pleasing result than the busy look created by using too many different flower varieties and colors.

HEIGHT AND SIZE RELATIONSHIPS

Consider plant height, leaf and flower size and its impact on groupings in the overall design and size of the bed or border

USING HEIGHT

Tall plants can provide a background for viewing lower growing plants but first determine how and where a flower bed or border will be viewed. For island beds that will be viewed from a multitude of locations place taller plants toward the middle of the bed, gradually stepping down heights toward the edge of the bed. For borders, place taller plants toward rear of bed so as not to block the view of shorter plants placed closer to the front of the border. Use lower growing plants near the edges of walkways.

NOTE ABOUT STAKING.

Be prepared to stake or provide additional support for taller growing herbaceous plants that might need it.

BLOCKING VIEWS

In some situations taller plants may be useful for effectively blocking out unsightly views of a neighboring property or can be used to hide structure or architectural flaw.

WIDE BEDS AND HEIGHT

Tall plants work better in wide beds. Generally speaking, the height of a background plant should not be more than two times the width of the bed.

Rose Mallow, *Hibiscus moscheutos*, page 69

FLOWER SHAPE AND SIZE

Annual and perennial flowers provide a vast array of sizes and shapes, from the tiny flowers of Sweet Alyssum to plate size flowers of hardy hibiscus. Mix it up for contrast and a more interesting design.

Consider Textures of Flowers and Foliage Too

When choosing plants for a grouping consider the textural look a plant provides.

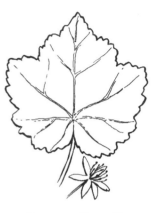

**Foamflower, *Tiarella cordifolia,*
page 75**

For instance, the big bold leaves of Hosta, the coarse texture of Iris or Yucca leaves or the fine texture of the foliage and flowers Coreopsis 'Moonbeam.' Fine textures provide a soft look to the garden, for instance, the small delicate white flowers of Foamflower that almost seem to float above its foliage provide a soft cloud-like look. Create interest and depth to groupings by combining two or more contrasting textures.

Variegation

In shady and dark areas of the garden consider using plants with variegated foliage, those plants that have white or yellow markings or speckling in their leaves (primarily due to a lack of chlorophyl in those areas of the leaf because of a genetic mutation or a virus). Using plants with variegated leaves will help brighten and liven up dark garden areas. Most plants with variegation in their leaves will however require some direct or bright sunlight for a few hours during the day or they might revert back to being all green.

**Garden Petunia, *Petunia x hybrida,*
page 81**

Don't be afraid to experiment. Try different combinations. See what works best in your flowerbeds, borders and garden situations. Good gardeners are always changing things in their garden, moving plants and trying different combinations. Remember, the use of annual flowers will provide lots of opportunities to change color schemes and try new plants. For many experienced gardeners a garden is a constant work in progress that's never ending. Use your imagination and have fun!

PLANTING TIPS

PLANTING AND MAINTENANCE

To achieve success, it's important to properly plant the selections and provide after planting care. Always make certain that the soil is properly prepared before planting, that all plants are planted at the proper depth and water thoroughly immediately after planting. Proper planting ensures strong vigorous growth, an abundance of flower production and increased disease and insect resistance.

Generally speaking, spring and early summer is traditionally the best time to do most major plantings of beds and borders. Planting perennials can begin in spring as soon as the ground thaws and is dry enough to work. Never work wet muddy soil, it will do damage to the soil structure. Perennials can also be successfully planted throughout the fall too. This gives them a chance to become better established and develop a larger healthier root system before they experience their first summer the following year.

Annual flowers, on the other hand are always planted in the spring, after the last frost date when all danger of frost at night is past. It's always a good idea to check with your local garden center or Cooperative Extension office for safe planting dates in your area and be prepare to protect tender annuals with a light cloth or plastic if an unexpected late frost does occur.

If possible try to choose cloudy overcast days or even a drizzly day to do major plantings. The lack of sun and cooler milder conditions will put less stress on transplants and will give the roots a chance to recover from damage incurred during the move from pots or flats or cell packs to their new home in the garden. However, if planting must be done on a sunny day be sure to water in plants immediately after planting. Providing a little temporary shade or protection from wind with a makeshift tent covered with a light cloth or white plastic film will help new plants get established faster.

Prior to planting and perhaps even before choosing plants, have a pH test done on the soil in the planting area. The pH test will determine how acidic or alkaline an existing soil is. Every plant has a desirable pH range it will grow best in. Once you know the pH of the soil you're working with then you can either choose plants that like the existing pH range or you can raise or lower it accordingly. Soil testing and advice on how to change and maintain the pH in your area can be obtained at any reputable local garden center or Cooperative Extension office.

PREPARING THE PLANTING AREA

There's basically two ways to prepare the soil of a planting bed. If it's a new area it would be best to prepare the entire area and then plant. If it's just a few plants that are being put into an existing bed or smaller

planting that are being tucked in here and there throughout the garden or landscape, then only the immediate area where the plants or group of plants are going to be planted should be worked. Start by clearing the area of any debris, dead plants, leaves, twigs rocks etc.

Determine if the existing soil is well-drained and free of compaction. If in doubt, it's always a good idea to add some organic matter like compost or peat moss (a mix of both is ideal) to improve the existing soil. A 1 to 2 inch layer of organic matter should be spread over the area along with a good organic fertilizer like Milorganite, Bone Meal, or Rock Phosphate (any one of these fertilizers will be all nutrients needed for the first 4-6 weeks) then mix into the soil. This material can be turned into the soil to a depth of a foot or more deep by hand with a spading fork or by using a roto-tiller. Break up any clods of soil and level the area flat with a level headed or bow rake. Now you're ready to plant.

Place and arrange plants according to the design, modifying the placement of individual plants to create a visually pleas-ing effect. Most plants have a good side and a less desirable side, so be sure to rotate and face plants accordingly. Once you're satisfied with the arrangement it's time to plant. Dig a hole beneath each plant that's as deep as the pot the plant came in. With potted plants like perennials and large annuals gently remove the plant from the pot by placing your fingers over the top of the pot, turning the pot and plant upside down and then, by tapping on the sides and the bottom of the pot, gently remove the pot by lift upward.

Once the pot is off, turn the plant right-side up and place plant in the hole, checking to make sure that the top of the soil ball is level with the surrounding soil of the bed. Now, back fill around the roots with the soil, pressing the soil firmly down around the plant.

Annuals and groundcovers are usually planted in mass plantings which requires a slightly different process. Using a trowel, transplanter or dibble, make a hole large enough to accommodate the young seedling or transplant's root system, gently placing and tucking it into the hole and firmly press the soil down around the plant. Space the next hole far enough away for the next plant to develop, follow spacing guidelines on plant labels or refer to reference tables for ideal spacing. Repeat the process until the entire bed is covered. Caution - Smaller plants in cell packs or smaller pots are delicate! Be careful not to accidentally break the more tender stems, leaves and shoots of these smaller plants.

Planting depth is important. Planting too deep will cause soil to come to far up the main stem at the base of the plant, possibly causing it to rot, causing an untimely death of the plant. When in doubt it is better to plant a little too shallow, the plant will eventually compensate for it by growing its root deeper. Always water plants in thoroughly immediately after planting.

Watch watering closely over the following weeks until plants develop their roots and become established. Water as needed when soil dries, checking soil moisture levels several times per week for the first few months. To help conserve moisture, keep soil and roots cool in the summer and prevent weed growth with a 1 to 2 inch thick layer of a natural organic mulch like pine or cedar bark, wood chips or pine needles.

Once again, be mindful of watering new plantings frequently until they've had time to develop new roots. As perennials become more established over the years, watering will be needed less frequently if the right plant has been selected for the conditions, properly planted and mulched, normal natural rainfall should sufficient with additional irrigation being needed only during summer drought. When you do water be sure to water deeply and thoroughly.

FERTILIZING

A few weeks after planting, apply a well-balanced fertilizer like Milorganite (a good deer repellent too), 5-10-5 or 10-10-10 every 4-6 weeks during the growing season or use one of the long lasting time-release fertilizers like Osmocote of Miracle Gro Shake and Feed. Always read and follow the label directions. Start fertilizing perennials in mid-March (around St. Patrick's Day) and continue through early fall when feeding stops. For annuals, the same well-balanced fertilizers should begin to be applied a few weeks after planting and every 4 - 6 weeks through the early fall.

PRUNING

Generally, the only regular pruning that most annual and perennial flowers will need at best is some periodical dead head-ing, the removal of spent flowers. This will encourage more flower development and will keep plantings looking their best. In the fall perennials can be cut back to the ground and annuals should be removed and discarded.

WEEDS

Keeping flowerbeds and borders weed free is important. Weeds rob nutrients and water while crowding out desirable plants. Weeds are also are great breeding grounds for all sorts of insect and disease problems. Weeding by hand is certainly acceptable but applying a 1 -2 inch layer of a mulch like wood chips, cedar or pine bark or any other natural organic mulch will not only suppress weed growth and eliminate a lot of work but will also conserve moisture, keep soil and roots cool and make the garden look neat and clean while adding organic matter to the soil. Organic mulches may need to be added to every few years since they do decompose over time.

PEST PROBLEMS

As with any living thing, plants can develop health problems too. Insects, fungus, bacteria and even viruses, as well as environmental and mechanical damage caused by man or nature can cause plant health to decline and can even lead to the ultimate death of the plant. In fact, declining health due to environmental factors, improper selection for site conditions, poor maintenance or soil compaction often leads to more serious insect, fungus, and bacterial problems. Weak plants are the most susceptible. Good health is the key to prevention.

Very simply, a healthy plant will not usually need treatments with pesticides, however, sometimes an unexpected health problem does occur. The proper selection of plants along with good maintenance, soil preparation, watering, fertilizing, pruning, etc. will go along way with preventing problems.

Plant ailments should be identified first and treated with the appropriate remedy as soon as possible. All plants should be looked at frequently, weekly if possible. A leisurely daily stroll around the grounds can be both enjoyable and purposeful in maintaining plant health. Look at and examine everything. Do spot checks, periodically looking at the undersides of leaves and along the trunks and branches. The more familiar you become with recognizing plants in good health the easier it will be able for you to recognize a plant that is having a problem, even if you can't identify it specifically on the spot.

Anything suspicious such as the development of spots on the leaves, any discoloration or the loss of overall vigor, as well as the presence of insects or unusual bumps or growths may be signs of a problem.

The first step is to properly identify the problem, then its cause, and then finally select the right cure. For this you may need the help and advice of experts. Bring samples to a horticultural expert at your local garden center or Cooperative Extension office for help. More often than not you've made large investments in time, money and effort to plan out your garden and landscape, don't let a simple problem get a foothold that could lead to great losses.

Deer Resistant Plants

What Deer Don't Like.

Using plants that deer don't like to eat, in other words deer resistant plants, may at first seem like the most logical and effective means of deer proofing your garden, however, it is not an exact science. What may work well in one place may prove ineffective in others. Hungry deer will try eating anything! Because deer behavior varies from location to location and depends primarily on the season, weather (snow cover), nutritional needs and the abundance or lack of abundance of their favorite foods, it is difficult to determine hard fast rules.

Documented evidence remains scarce, however experimentation through guided trial and error will eventually lead to a deer proof garden. Luckily, results from the trial and errors of others is now available here. Good planning and a little patience is all you'll need to have a deer proof flowerbeds and borders .

Native Plants

Perhaps at first, the most logical method of creating deer-proof flower beds and borders is to mimic nature. By observing and noting those native plants that deer leave alone in your area you'll be able to draw some conclusions. Experience has shown that once a native plant is found to be immune to deer damage, closely related members of that plant's family usually prove to be resistant as well. For example, plants in the Ranunculus family (Ranunculaceae) includes our native Buttercup and Marsh Marigold (Caltha) as well as many cultivated members such as Columbine, Delphinium and Winter Aconite to mention just a few, all of which are resistant to deer damage. As a result, if you find a particular native plant is resistant to deer damage, identify it to determine what

Daffodil, *Narcissus*, page 85

family it belongs to and select other members for trial in your landscape or garden. For help with identification, bring a sample to a horticulturist at a local garden center, Cooperative Extension office or botanic garden.

PLANT CHARACTERISTICS THAT DETERMINE RESISTANCE:

TOXICITY

Toxicity is perhaps one of the most common reasons for deer to leave a particular plant and its family members unscathed in your landscape or garden. The above is a good example. Members of the Ranunculus family contain members that are very poisonous to deer and other grazing animals, thus leaving the plants untouched more often than not. Daffodils are another good example of plants that are left alone by deer and rodents (especially squirrels). But there is no need for alarm. In most cases, large quantities of foliage and other plant parts would have to be ingested to have a toxic reaction.

Lavender, *Lavandula officinalis*, page 87

A word of caution however, whenever considering a new plant. It is always a good idea to find out about its relative toxicity when being handled since some plants may give off toxins when handled and proper precautions should be taken when handling, such as wearing gloves and long sleeves.

AROMA

Aromatic foliage is more often than not shunned by deer. In fact many of the commonly cultivated herbs used for cooking and preparing dishes as well as those used in aromatherapy and for other medicinal purposes, are resistant to deer damage. Often, these herbs primarily serve a threefold purpose in the landscape and garden. First, they are deer resistant, they are also used as a flavoring, fragrance or medicine, all while providing ornamental value as an added benefit in the landscape and garden. Examples of deer resistant plants with aromatic foliage include Basil, Lavender, Thyme, Yarrow.

FUZZY FOLIAGE

There is perhaps nothing more disagreeable to deer than a mouthful of fuzz. Deer just seem to steer clear of foliage that have a pubescent covering. The short soft hairs that cover the leaves of certain plants such as Lamb's Ears, Dead Nettle, Rose Campion and Black-Eyed Susan provide the plant with a characteristic that make them shunned by deer. It is safe to say that any other plants that have fuzz covered leaves that you come across will provide resistance.

Dead Nettle, *Lamium maculatum*, page 52, 56

PRICKLY PARTS

Although these characteristics are found predominantly in woody stemmed trees and shrubs, thorns, spines and needles provide good clues for determining a plant's resistance to deer damage. Hard, needle type foliage found on many evergreens such as Spruce, Pine, and Junipers provide very good protection from deer damage, as do the thorny stems and branches of Barberry, English Hawthorn, and Japanese Flowering Quince. Deer will also avoid the hard, prickly edged leaves of American and English Holly and Leucothoe as well as Oregon Grape Holly. However, deer have been known to be carefully selective about consuming the soft succulent buds and flow-

American Holly, *Ilex opaca*

ers from plants such as Roses and Hawthorn while leaving the thorny covered stems and branched alone. Perhaps the additional protection provided by plastic netting or a fence or a trellis would be best.

MAKING THE RIGHT SELECTIONS

The remainder of this book provides a guide for choosing the right plants. The lists are made up of plants that have been known to have a resistancy to deer browsing in many locations throughout the country. Remember, a plant's resistance may vary due to location, weather, season, environmental stress factors and a deer's stage of physical development.

CONCENTRATE ON USING THE PLANTS DEER HAVE BEEN KNOWN TO DISLIKE.

There are many plants that deer will leave alone. New landscapes and gardens, with a little extra work, can be designed and planned to use only those plants known to be deer proof. For those whose landscapes and gardens already exist, perhaps a transition period makes sense. Plans can be made for renovating by adding deer proof plants while removing their favorites, all the while employing the use of repellents as needed to prevent devastation.

CHOOSE THE PLANTS FOR THE CONDITIONS OF THE LOCATION THEY WILL BE GROWING IN (sun light, soil, water).

Besides being deer proof, the plants chosen must be right for the area they are to be planted in. Be sure to consider how much sun the spot gets during the entire day. Consider whether the area is primarily exposed to Full Sun (direct sun all day), Deep Shade (no direct sun at all), or Partial Shade/Sun (morning, mid or late afternoon sun only, etc.).

ALSO CONSIDER THE TYPE OF SOIL THAT EXISTS IN THE AREA.

Is it dominantly sandy, clay or loam? Does the area drains well or do puddles of water persist, or does the area stay soggy wet for extended periods, a day or more? Will the area be irrigated or will these plants need to depend on natural rainfall only? All are important considerations when selecting plant that will grow and thrive.

CHOOSE PLANTS THAT WORK WELL TOGETHER (flower and foliage color, texture, size)

Finally, choose plants that will look good together. Like choosing what you wear every day, colors textures and proper fit or size are combined for a pleasing effect. Consider not only flower color when choosing a flowering plant, but keep in mind foliage color as well.

Plants provide variations in texture as well. Large and/or pointed leaves provide a coarse look while many tiny, rounded, or smooth edged and small fine leaves provide softer textures.

And last, but not least, choose the right size plant for the area. Always consider a plants mature height whether selecting

shade trees or plants for a flower border. Generally, larger plants are used in the background while shorter low growing plants are best used up in front and as edging. The overall goal is to create harmony. Combinations of colors, textures and sizes that look good together. (Refer to Chapter 3, Designing Flower Beds and Borders for more advice and design tips.)

A Deer Good-Bye !

Always remember that one of the greatest things about gardening is that it's not an exact science. There's plenty of room for experimentation, improvement and learning your own way of doing it. A garden is a constant work in progress. Don't be afraid to move plants, when the mood strikes you, or rip out, discard and replace plants that are not working or performing to your liking or simply died. Good gardeners do this all the time and yes, even the best gardeners sometimes kill a plant or two. Learn from your mistakes and move on. When in doubt, it always pays to consult with experts or fellow gardening enthusiasts. Horticulturists are always happy to help and share - it's their nature. Sometimes getting together with fellow gardening enthusiasts

in your area to share what works and doesn't when it comes to deer resistant plants and repellents can reveal some very valuable advice and tips that will work for you. By and large, don't worry, have fun, enjoy the rewards and just do it!

Now I hope you're well on your way to having a beautiful deer-proof flower beds and borders!

Pachysandra, Japanese Spurge,
***Pachysandra terminalis*, page 56**

PLANTS RESISTANT TO DEER BROWSING BY LATIN NAME

Plants on this list have been found to be least preferred in varying degrees by deer. This does not mean that they will not feed on them. Plants will have varying levels of vulnerability depending on a number of factors including local deer population density, severity of weather and abundancy of natural food sources. If natural or other food sources are available and/or abundundant, these plants will probably be overlooked by deer.

However, deer can often be unpredictable and have a tendency to "browse" on plants that are in their feeding "comfort" areas while the same plant may be left untouched in other areas so their may be variations in feeding patterns within a given piece of property, garden or landscape.

ANNUAL FLOWERS

LATIN NAME	COMMON NAME
Agastache foeniculum	Anise Hyssop (p91)
Ageratum houstonianum	Ageratum or Flossflower (p77)
Alternanthera ficoidea	Joseph's Coat
Angelonia angustifolia	Angelonia
Antirrhinum majus	Snapdragon (p77)
Arctotis stoechadifolia	African Daisy
Asperula orientalis	Annual Woodruff
Begonia semperflorens	Wax Begonia
Begonia x tuberhybrida	Tuberous Begonia
Bidens ferulifolia	Bidens
Brachycome iberidifolia	Swan River Daisy
Brugmansia versicolor	Angels Trumpets
Calibrachoa (hybrids)	Million Bells
Campanula medium	Canterbury Bells
Capsicum annuum	Ornamental Pepper
Catharanthus roseus	Annual Vinca
Clarkia hybridus	Clarkia
Cleome hasslerana	Spider Flower
Consolida ambigua	Annual Larkspur
Cynoglossum amabile	Chinese Forget-Me-Not

LATIN NAME	COMMON NAME
Datura meteloides	Downy Thornapple
Dianthus barbatus	Sweet William
Emilia javanica	Tassel Flower
Euphorbia marginata	Snow-On-The-Mountain
Eustoma grandilflorum	Lisianthus
Evolvulus glomeratus	Evolvulus, Blue Daze
Felicia echinata	Blue Marguerite
Gaillardia pulchella	Blanket Flower
Gomphrena globosa	Globe Amaranth
Gypsophila repens	Baby's Breath
Helianthus	Sunflowers
Helichrysum bracteatum	Straw Flower
Heliotropium arborescens	Heliotrope (p78)
Hunnemania fumarifolia	Mexican Tulip Poppy
Hypoestes phyllostachya	Polka-dot Plant
Iberis umbellata	Candytuft
Ipomoea alba	Moonflower (p78)
Ipomoea purpurea	Morning Glory (p79)
Kochia scoparia	Burning Bush

LATIN NAME	COMMON NAME
Lantana camara(and montevidensis)	Lantana
Lobelia erinus	Lobelia (p79)
Lobularia maritima	Sweet Alyssum
Matthiola incana	Common Stock
Melampodium paludosum	Butter Daisy
Mimulus cupreus	Monkey Flower (p80)
Mirabilis jalapa	Four O' Clocks (p80)
Nemesia strumosa	Carnival Flower
Nierembergia hippomanica	Cup Flower
Nigella damascena	Love-In-A-Mist
Osteospermum (hybrids)	African Daisy Hybrids
Oxypetalum caeruleum	Southern Star
Pelargonium x hortorum	Common Geranium
Pennisetum sp.	Annual Fountain Grass
Penstemon x gloxinoides	Hybrid Penstemon
Pentas lanceolata	Pentas, Egyptian Star Flower
Perilla frutescens	Beefstake Plant
Petunia x hybrida	Garden Petunia (p81)
Phlox drummondii	Annual Phlox
Polygonum capitatum	Pinkhead Knotweed

LATIN NAME	COMMON NAME
Salvia (all varieties)	Sages (p81)
Tagetes (all varieties)	Marigolds (p82)
Thymophylla tenuiloba	Dahlberg Daisy
Tithonia rotundifolia	Mexican Sunflower
Tropaeolum majus	Nasturtium (p82)
Verbena bonariensis	Verbena
Verbena rigida	Verbena Vervain
Xeranthemum annuum	Immortelle
Zinnia angustifolia	Star Zinnia
Zinnia haageana	Mexican Zinnia
Zinnia linearis	Narrowleaf Zinnia

PERENNIAL FLOWERS

LATIN NAME	COMMON NAME
Achillea filipendula	Fernleaf Yarrow (p62)
Achillea millefolium	Common Yarrow
Aconitum sp.	Monkshood (p62)
Agastache cana	Mosquito Plant
Alyssum saxatile	Golden Alyssum
Amsonia tabernaemontana	Eastern Bluestar
Anemone hupehensis japonica	Japanese Anemone
Anthemis tinctoria	Gold Marguerite
Aquilegia vulgaris	Columbine
Arabis sp.	Rock Cress (p63)
Armeria maritima	Sea Thrift
Artemisia schmidtiana	Wormwood (p63)
Asarum europaeum	European Wild Ginger
Asclepias tuberosa	Butterfly Milkweed (p64)
Aster novi-belgi	New York Asters (p64)
Astilbe x arendsii	Astilbe (p65)
Aubretia deltoidea	Purple Rock-Cress (p65)
Aurinia saxatilis	Basket of Gold (p66)
Baptisia tinctoria	False Indigo
Bergenia sp.	Bergenia
Boltonia asteroides	Boltonia

LATIN NAME	COMMON NAME
Camassia sp.	Camassia
Campanula sp.	Bellflower
Centaurea cineraria	Dusty Miller
Centranthus ruber	Red Valerian
Chelone obliqua	Pink Turtle Head
Chrysanthemum	Mums
Cimicifuga racemosa	Snakeroot
Cirsium japnicum	Sea Thistle
Coreopsis lanceolata	Lance Coreopsis (p66)
Coreopsis sp.	Tickseed
Corydalis lutea	Fumewort
Delphinium elatum	Larkspur
Dicentra sp.	Bleeding Heart
Dictamnus albus	White Gas Plant
Echinacea purpurea	Purple Coneflower (p67)
Echinops ritro	Globe Thistle
Eryngium sp.	Sea Holly
Filipendula ulmaria	Meadowsweet (p68)
Gaillardia aristata	Gaillardia
Geranium	Cranesbill (p68)
Geum coccineum	Geum

LATIN NAME	COMMON NAME
Gypsophila paniculata	Baby's Breath
Helenium autumnale	Sneezeweed (p69)
Helleborus orientalis	Lenten-rose
Hemerocallis	Daylily
Hesperis matronalis	Dame's Rocket
Hibiscus moscheutos	Rose Mallow (p69)
Hypericum sp.	St. John's Wort
Inula helenium	Elecampane
Iris siberica & ensata	Siberian & Japanese Iris
Kniphofia uvaria	Red Hot Poker, Torch Lily
Lavandula angustifolia	Lavender
Liatris sp.	Gayfeathers
Limonium latifolium	Sea Lavender
Linum perenne	Perennial Flax
Lupinus perennis	Wild Lupine
Lychnis chalcedonica	Maltese Cross

LATIN NAME	COMMON NAME
Lychnis coronaria	Rose Campion (p70)
Lysimachia clethroides	Japanese Loosestrife (p70)
Lythrum salicaria	Purple Loosestrife (p71)
Macleaya cordata	Plume Poppy
Matteuccia pennsylvanica	Ostrich Fern
Mentha sp.	Mints
Monarda didyma	Beebalm (p71)
Myosotis scorpioides & sylvatica	Forget-Me-Nots
Nepeta sp.	Catmint
Oenethera sp.	Sundrops or Evening Primrose
Paeonia sp. & hybrids	Peony (p72)
Papaver orientale	Oriental Poppy
Perovskia atriplcifolia	Russian Sage (p72)
Physostegia virginiana	Obedient Plant
Platycodon grandiflorus	Balloon Flower
Polemonium caeruleum	Jacob's Ladder (p73)
Polygonatum sp.	Solomon's Seal
Primula x polyantha	Primrose

LATIN NAME	COMMON NAME
Pulmonaria sp.	Lungwort
Rudbeckia maxima	Black-Eyed Susan (p73)
Salvia sp.	Perennial Salvia
Santolina chamaecyparissus	Lavender-cotton
Saponaria ocymoides	Rock Soapwort
Scabiosa caucasia	Caucasian Scabious
Solidago sp. & hybrids	Goldenrods (p74)
Stachys byzantina	Lamb's Ears (p74)
Thalictrum flavum	Meadow-Rue
Thermopsis caroliniana	False Lupin
Thymus vulgaris	Common Thyme (p75)
Tiarella cordifolia	Foamflower (p75)
Trillium undulatum	Painted Trillium
Veronica incana & longifolia	Speedwell
Viola sp.	Violets & Johnny Jump-ups
Yucca filamentosa	Adam's Needle (p76)

BIENNIALS

LATIN NAME	**COMMON NAME**
Digitalis purpurea	Foxglove
Myosotis alpestris	Hardy Forget-Me-Not

BULBS

Allium sp.	Ornamental Onions (p83)
Chionodoxa luciliae	Glory-of-the-Snow
Colchicum autumnale	Autumn Crocus
Crocus	Crocus
Eranthis hyemalis	Winter Aconite
Fritillaria sp.	Crown Imperial (Fritllary) (p83)
Galanthus elwesii	Giant Snowdrop
Galanthus nivalis	Common Snowdrop (p84)
Leucojum vernum	Spring Snowflake
Lycoris sp.	Resurrection Lily
Muscari botryoides	Common Grape Hyacinth (p84)
Narcissus	Narcissus, Daffodils and Jonquils (p85)
Puschkinia scilloides	Striped Squill
Scilla siberica	Siberian Squill (p85)

HERBS

LATIN NAME	COMMON NAME
Allium shoenoprasum	Chives (p86)
Anethum graveolens	Dill
Angelica archangelica	Angelica (p86)
Anthemis nobilis	Chamomile
Artimisia dracunculus	Artemisia
Borago officinalis	Borage Burnet
Chrysanthemum parthenium	Feverfew
Foeniculum vulgare	Fennel
Hyssopus officinalis	Hyssop (p87)
Lavendula officianalis	Lavender (p87)
Levisticum officinalis	Lovage
Marrubium vulgare	Horehound (p88)
Melissa officinalis	Lemon Balm (p88)
Mentha piperita	Peppermint (p89)
Mentha pulegium	European Pennyroyal (p89)
Mentha spicata	Spearmint

LATIN NAME	COMMON NAME
Nepeta cataria	Catmint (p90)
Ocimum basilicum	Basil (p90)
Origanum vulgare	Oregano
Petroselinum crispum	Parsley
Pimpinalla anisum	Anise (p91)
Rosmarinus officinalis	Rosemary
Ruta graveolens	Rue (p91)
Salvia officinalis	Sage (p92)
Satureja montana	Savory (p92)
Symphytum officinale	Comfrey
Tanacetum vulgare	Tansy
Teucrium chamaedrys	Germander
Thymus vulgaris	Thyme
Verbascum thapsus	Mullein

ORNAMENTAL GRASSES

LATIN NAME	COMMON NAME
Acorus calamus	Sweetflag or Gardener's Grass
Calamagrostis x acutiflora	Reed Grass
Carex sp.	Sedges
Festuca ovina "glauca"	Blue Fescue
Miscanthus sp.	Silver Grasses
Pennisetum sp.	Fountain Grasses

PERENNIAL GROUNDCOVERS

LATIN NAME	COMMON NAME
Ajuga reptans	Bugleweed (p54)
Alchemilla vulgaris	Lady's Mantle
Arctostaphyllos	Bearberry (p54)
Asarum europaeum	European Wild Ginger

LATIN NAME	COMMON NAME
Bergenia crassifolia	Bergenia
Cerastium tomentosum	Snow-in-Summer
Convallaria majus	Lily-of-the-Valley (p55)
Cotoneaster horizontalis	Rockspray Cotoneaster
Epimedium grandiflorum	Barrenwort (p55)
Euonymus fortunei	Wintercreeper
Ferns	Ferns
Galium odoratum	Sweet Woodruff
Juniperus horizontalis	Creeping Juniper
Lamium maculatum	Dead Nettle (p56)
Pachysandra terminalis	Pachysandra, Japanese Spurge (p56)
Potentilla	Cinquefoils
Pulmonaria officinalis	Common Lungwort
Santolina chamaecyparissus	Santolina, Lavender-cotton (p57)
Sedum sp.	Sedums
Sempervirens tectorum	Hens-and-Chicks (p57)
Vancouveria hexandra	American Barrenwort
Vinca minor	Periwinkle, Myrtle (p58)

VINES

LATIN NAME	COMMON NAME
Akebia quinata	Fiveleaf Akebia (p59)
Campsis radicans	Trumpet Vine (p59)
Celastrus scandens	Bittersweet (p60)
Clematis	Clematis
Hedera helix	English Ivy
Lonicera x heckrottii	Goldflame Honeysuckle
Parthenocissus tricuspdidata	Boston Ivy
Parthenocissus quinquefolia	Virginia Creeper
Polygonum aubertii	Silver Lace Vine (p60)
Vitis labrusca	Fox Grape Vine (p61)
Wisteria floribunda	Japanese Wisteria (p61)

Ajuga reptans
BUGLEWEED

DEER ATTRACTION: Rarely.
HABIT: Low, fast spreading ground cover.
SIZE: 4–12" tall.
LEAVES: Evergreen, 4" long, round to oval. Foliage is available in several
colors that include green, bronze, deep purple, and variegated.
FLOWERS: Compact, 2–4" upright spikes that appear in May through
June and are available in blue, white, and purplish red.
TEXTURE: Medium.
CULTURE: Full sun to shade. Adapts to most well drained soils.
LANDSCAPE/ GARDEN VALUE: Primarily used as a ground cover.
HARDINESS: Zone 2.
SPECIAL CHARACTERISTICS: A member of the mint family. Fancy
varieties may freely self seed the area they are planted in; how-
ever, seedlings may not look like parents but will usually revert
back to species. Therefore, unwanted seedlings may need to be
selectively removed or the area may need to be replanted every few
years.

Arctostaphyllos uva-ursi
BEARBERRY

DEER ATTRACTION: Rarely.
HABIT: Low growing, evergreen ground cover.
SIZE: 6–12" tall and 2–4' wide.
LEAVES: Evergreen, 1/2" wide, oblong to round. Very shiny, dark green on
top, lighter beneath. Turns red to bronze in the fall and winter.
FLOWERS: Tiny whitish pink, 1/6" long bell-shaped flowers appear in April
and early May.
TEXTURE: Fine.
CULTURE: Full sun or partial shade. Adapts well to almost any well
drained soil. Prefers acidic soils (pH of 4.5–5.5) and tolerates salt
and seaside conditions. Does not like fertilization and excessive
watering. Seems to thrive on neglect.
LANDSCAPE/ GARDEN VALUE: Primarily used as a ground cover.
HARDINESS: Zone 2.
NATIVE HABITAT: Europe, Asia, and North America.
SPECIAL CHARACTERISTICS: Good fall color. One of the best ground covers
for use where deer browsing is a severe problem.

Convallaria majalis
LILY-OF-THE-VALLEY

DEER ATTRACTION: Rarely.
HABIT: Low, spreading ground cover.
SIZE: 8" high.
LEAVES: 8" long, 1–3" wide, oval. Leaves die to ground completely in fall.
FLOWERS: Upright spikes with white, 1/4" wide, waxy, hanging, bell-like flowers that are pleasantly fragrant and appear in mid–May through mid–June.
TEXTURE: Medium.
CULTURE: Thrives in shade. Prefers rich, moist, well drained soil. Responds well to yearly application of an organic fertilizer in spring, but once established, beds require little or no other maintenance.
LANDSCAPE/ GARDEN VALUE: Good ground cover for shade.
HARDINESS: Zone 2.
NATIVE HABITAT: Europe, Asia, and Eastern North America.
SPECIAL CHARACTERISTICS: Low maintenance ground cover. A pink flowering variety, "Rosea" is also available. Propagated and grown from rhizomes (modified underground stem).

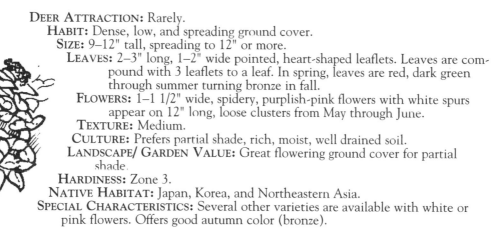

Epimedium grandiflorum
BARRENWORT

DEER ATTRACTION: Rarely.
HABIT: Dense, low, and spreading ground cover.
SIZE: 9–12" tall, spreading to 12" or more.
LEAVES: 2–3" long, 1–2" wide pointed, heart-shaped leaflets. Leaves are compound with 3 leaflets to a leaf. In spring, leaves are red, dark green through summer turning bronze in fall.
FLOWERS: 1–1 1/2" wide, spidery, purplish-pink flowers with white spurs appear on 12" long, loose clusters from May through June.
TEXTURE: Medium.
CULTURE: Prefers partial shade, rich, moist, well drained soil.
LANDSCAPE/ GARDEN VALUE: Great flowering ground cover for partial shade.
HARDINESS: Zone 3.
NATIVE HABITAT: Japan, Korea, and Northeastern Asia.
SPECIAL CHARACTERISTICS: Several other varieties are available with white or pink flowers. Offers good autumn color (bronze).

Lamium maculatum
DEAD NETTLE

DEER ATTRACTION: Rarely.
HABIT: Dense, low, and spreading ground cover.
SIZE: 6–12" tall, spreading to 18" or more.
LEAVES: 1 1/2–2 1/2" long, oval, heart-shaped, crinkled with serrated edge. Leaves are green with silvery white splotches.
FLOWERS: 1–2" long, purplish-pink flowers appear throughout the summer.
TEXTURE: Medium.
CULTURE: Prefers partial shade and rich, moist, well drained soil.
LANDSCAPE/ GARDEN VALUE: Great flowering ground cover for partial shade.
HARDINESS: Zone 2.
NATIVE HABITAT: Europe.
SPECIAL CHARACTERISTICS: Blooms throughout most of the summer. White flowering varieties are available. May become invasive. Silvery, light colored foliage lightens up dark, shady areas and contrasts well with dark green evergreens. An attractive background for taller and colorful plants.

Pachysandra terminalis
PACHYSANDRA OR JAPANESE SPURGE

DEER ATTRACTION: Rarely.
HABIT: Low spreading ground cover.
SIZE: 6–12" tall, spreading to 18" or more.
LEAVES: 2–3" dark green, shiny, and deeply serrated oval. Foliage remains through winter.
FLOWERS: 2–3" white, upright spikes appear in early May, but not very showy.
TEXTURE: Medium.
CULTURE: Shade to part sun. Prefers rich, moist, well drained, slightly acidic soil but will adapt well to a wide variety of locations except constant hot, dry, sunny areas, but will tolerate dry shade. Plants are stoloniferous and can spread rapidly when fertilized regularly.
LANDSCAPE/ GARDEN VALUE: Great ground cover for shady areas, especially under and around trees and shrubs where competition from roots may cause soil to stay dry near the surface.
HARDINESS: Zone 5. **NATIVE HABITAT:** Japan.
SPECIAL CHARACTERISTICS: Produces white, inconspicuous fruits-berries in fall. Probably the most commonly found ground cover. Despite its ubiquitous nature, pachysandra is one of the most dependable ground covers for use in the deer resistant garden or land-

Santolina chamaecyparissus
LAVENDER-COTTON

DEER ATTRACTION: Rarely.
HABIT: Low, shrubby.
SIZE: 1 1/2–2' tall and wide.
LEAVES: 1/2–3/4" long, lance-like, aromatic and silvery gray.
FLOWERS: Small yellow flowers appear in 1/2–3/4" clusters in July and August.
TEXTURE: Fine.
CULTURE: Full sun. Prefers poor sandy or gravely soils. Tolerates hot and very dry conditions.
LANDSCAPE/ GARDEN VALUE: Use as a ground cover or border edge. Great for rock and wall gardens.
HARDINESS: Zones 6–7.
NATIVE HABITAT: Southern Europe.
SPECIAL CHARACTERISTICS: Its aromatic foliage acts as a deer repellent. Herbal uses include its household use as a moth repellent and its oil being used to make perfume.

Sempervirens tectorum
HENS-AND-CHICKS

DEER ATTRACTION: Rarely.
HABIT: Very low, ground hugging ground cover.
SIZE: 8–12" tall and wide.
LEAVES: 1/4–1/2" bluntly pointed ovals that tightly circle its center forming a densely crowded rosette of grayish green leaves, often red tipped, 3–4" across.
FLOWERS: 3/4–1" across, clusters of pink-purple flowers appear on 8–12" hairy stalks infrequently throughout the summer.
TEXTURE: Coarse.
CULTURE: Full sun. Likes hot, dry, poor soils. Plants multiply rapidly by forming smaller plants at their base, therefore forming continuously spreading mats of dense rosettes.
LANDSCAPE/ GARDEN VALUE: Excellent ground cover for hot, dry, sunny areas. Suitable for rock gardens. Use in crevices of rock walls and between stones in paths.
HARDINESS: Zone 4.
NATIVE HABITAT: Europe and Asia.
SPECIAL CHARACTERISTICS: Cultivated since the 16th century, Hens-and-Chicks are very hardy and durable and can be effective in areas where the extremes of sun, heat, and dryness won't allow anything else to cover the ground adequately.

Vinca minor

PERIWINKLE OR MYRTLE

DEER ATTRACTION: Rarely.
HABIT: Low, spreading ground cover.
SIZE: 4–6" tall.
LEAVES: 2" long, dark green, shiny ovals.
FLOWERS: 3/4" across, lavender-blue flowers in late April.
TEXTURE: Medium.
CULTURE: Full sun to deep shade. Will tolerate almost any but the poorest soils. Reproduces easily since stems root readily where it comes in contact with soil.
LANDSCAPE/ GARDEN VALUE: Good ground cover for almost any area.
Hardiness: Zone 4.
NATIVE HABITAT: Europe and Western Asia.
SPECIAL CHARACTERISTICS: Like pachysandra, it's rather ubiquitous in gardens and landscapes, however, its resistance to deer browsing is often unsurpassed and therefore is of value in the deer resistant garden or landscape.

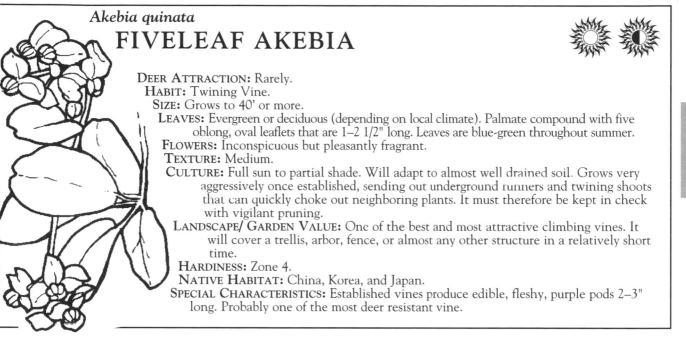

Akebia quinata
FIVELEAF AKEBIA

DEER ATTRACTION: Rarely.
HABIT: Twining Vine.
SIZE: Grows to 40' or more.
LEAVES: Evergreen or deciduous (depending on local climate). Palmate compound with five oblong, oval leaflets that are 1–2 1/2" long. Leaves are blue-green throughout summer.
FLOWERS: Inconspicuous but pleasantly fragrant.
TEXTURE: Medium.
CULTURE: Full sun to partial shade. Will adapt to almost well drained soil. Grows very aggressively once established, sending out underground runners and twining shoots that can quickly choke out neighboring plants. It must therefore be kept in check with vigilant pruning.
LANDSCAPE/ GARDEN VALUE: One of the best and most attractive climbing vines. It will cover a trellis, arbor, fence, or almost any other structure in a relatively short time.
HARDINESS: Zone 4.
NATIVE HABITAT: China, Korea, and Japan.
SPECIAL CHARACTERISTICS: Established vines produce edible, fleshy, purple pods 2–3" long. Probably one of the most deer resistant vine.

Campsis radicans
TRUMPET VINE

DEER ATTRACTION: Occasionally.
HABIT: Clinging, shrubby vine.
SIZE: Grows to over 50' or more.
LEAVES: Deciduous, brilliant green compound leaf, 6–8" long with 9–11 leaflets that are 1 1/4–1 1/2" long with serrated edges.
FLOWERS: 2–4" long, orange, trumpet shaped flowers grouped in clusters of 4–12 that begin to appear in July and continue through September.
TEXTURE: Medium.
CULTURE: Full sun and almost any type of soil. A very tough, vigorous grower with little or minimum care. Often spreads by underground runners.
LANDSCAPE/ GARDEN VALUE: A vigorous flowering vine for covering a trellis, arbor, fence, wall, or other structure.
HARDINESS: Zone 4.
NATIVE HABITAT: Mid-Atlantic of United States, south to Florida and west to Texas.
SPECIAL CHARACTERISTICS: Holds to objects using aerial rootlets (holdfasts) that cling to structures. Handling leaves or flowers may cause dermatitis.

Celastrus scandens
BITTERSWEET

DEER ATTRACTION: Seldomly.
HABIT: Twining vine.
SIZE: Grows to 20' or more.
LEAVES: Deciduous, 2–4" long, pointed, oval. Shiny, bright green in summer, yellow fall color.
FLOWERS: Inconspicuous.
TEXTURE: Medium in leaf, coarse when leafless.
CULTURE: Full sun to partial shade. Adapts to almost any soil. Grows very vigorously when planted in good soil.
LANDSCAPE/ GARDEN VALUE: A very fast growing, twining vine that is usually used or allowed to ramble over fences, walls, rock piles, dead or live tree trunks, or any other structure, or eyesore.
HARDINESS: Zone 3.
NATIVE HABITAT: Canada, south to Mexico and east of the Rockies.
SPECIAL CHARACTERISTICS: Yellow fruit with crimson seeds appear in October that provide ornamental value and is often harvested and used in dried flower arrangements.

Polygonum aubertii
SILVER LACE VINE

DEER ATTRACTION: Occasionally.
HABIT: Twining vine.
SIZE: Grows to 35' or more.
LEAVES: Deciduous, 1 1/2–2 1/2" long, oblong, oval with undulating leaf margin. Leaves are bright green through summer, new growth is reddish bronze turning to green.
FLOWERS: Small, 1/4" wide, fragrant white flowers appear in short panicles in July through September.
TEXTURE: Medium in leaf, otherwise coarse.
CULTURE: Full sun or shade. Adapts to almost any soil. Tolerates very dry soils. Once established it is a vigorous grower.
LANDSCAPE/ GARDEN VALUE: A good, quick growing vine that adapts well to poor conditions where other vines fail to thrive. It will quickly cover a fence, arbor, or any other structure.
HARDINESS: Zone 4.
NATIVE HABITAT: China.
SPECIAL CHARACTERISTICS: Susceptible to Japanese Beetle damage.

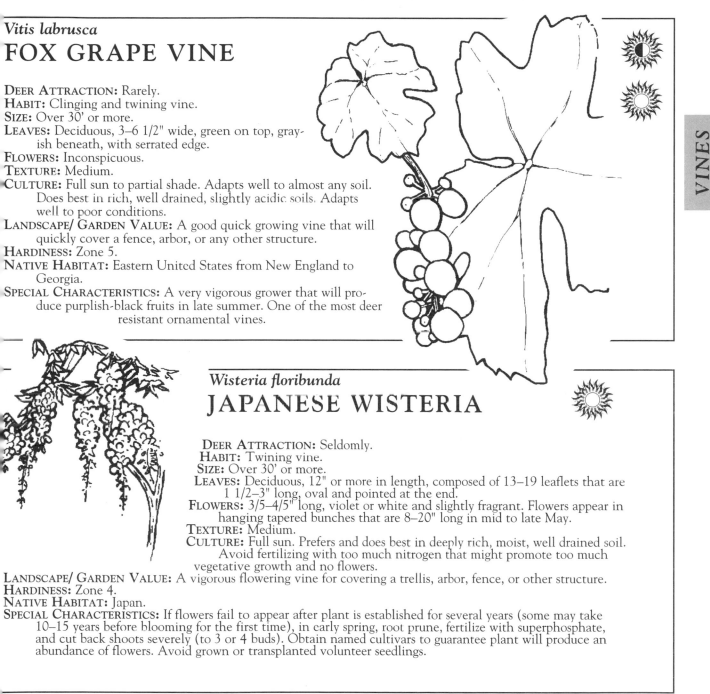

Vitis labrusca
FOX GRAPE VINE

DEER ATTRACTION: Rarely.
HABIT: Clinging and twining vine.
SIZE: Over 30' or more.
LEAVES: Deciduous, 3–6 1/2" wide, green on top, grayish beneath, with serrated edge.
FLOWERS: Inconspicuous.
TEXTURE: Medium.
CULTURE: Full sun to partial shade. Adapts well to almost any soil. Does best in rich, well drained, slightly acidic soils. Adapts well to poor conditions.
LANDSCAPE/ GARDEN VALUE: A good quick growing vine that will quickly cover a fence, arbor, or any other structure.
HARDINESS: Zone 5.
NATIVE HABITAT: Eastern United States from New England to Georgia.
SPECIAL CHARACTERISTICS: A very vigorous grower that will produce purplish-black fruits in late summer. One of the most deer resistant ornamental vines.

Wisteria floribunda
JAPANESE WISTERIA

DEER ATTRACTION: Seldomly.
HABIT: Twining vine.
SIZE: Over 30' or more.
LEAVES: Deciduous, 12" or more in length, composed of 13–19 leaflets that are 1 1/2–3" long, oval and pointed at the end.
FLOWERS: 3/5–4/5" long, violet or white and slightly fragrant. Flowers appear in hanging tapered bunches that are 8–20" long in mid to late May.
TEXTURE: Medium.
CULTURE: Full sun. Prefers and does best in deeply rich, moist, well drained soil. Avoid fertilizing with too much nitrogen that might promote too much vegetative growth and no flowers.
LANDSCAPE/ GARDEN VALUE: A vigorous flowering vine for covering a trellis, arbor, fence, or other structure.
HARDINESS: Zone 4.
NATIVE HABITAT: Japan.
SPECIAL CHARACTERISTICS: If flowers fail to appear after plant is established for several years (some may take 10–15 years before blooming for the first time), in early spring, root prune, fertilize with superphosphate, and cut back shoots severely (to 3 or 4 buds). Obtain named cultivars to guarantee plant will produce an abundance of flowers. Avoid grown or transplanted volunteer seedlings.

Achillea millefolium
YARROW

DEER ATTRACTION: Rarely.
HABIT: Upright.
SIZE: 2–3' tall, 15–24" wide.
LEAVES: 6–8" long, feathery green.
FLOWERS: Tiny white or pink flowers appear in 1 1/2–2" clusters from mid–July through mid–September.
TEXTURE: Fine.
CULTURE: Full sun. Does best in well drained, average to poor soil. Very tolerant of hot, dry conditions.
LANDSCAPE/ GARDEN VALUE: Perennial or mixed beds and borders especially where little or no irrigation is available.
HARDINESS: Zone 3.
NATIVE HABITAT: Europe.
SPECIAL CHARACTERISTICS: Hybrid cultivars called "Galaxy Hybrids" are available that offer deep red, amber, and salmon color variations.

Aconitum carmichaelii
MONKSHOOD

DEER ATTRACTION: Rarely.
HABIT: Upright.
SIZE: 4–6' tall, 18–24" wide.
LEAVES: 2–3" wide, 3 lobed, leathery dark green leaves, similar to *Delphinium elatum* (p76).
FLOWERS: Blue, violet, lavender, depending on cultivar, appear on 6" compact spikes in August and September.
TEXTURE: Medium.
CULTURE: Full sun, but will do quite well in partial shade. Prefers moist, well drained soil. Will not tolerate hot, dry conditions too well. Often needs to be staked.
LANDSCAPE/ GARDEN VALUE: A tall growing perennial, use in perennial or mixed borders as a background plant. Best used in masses. Contrasts well with yellow and white flowering plants.
HARDINESS: Zone 3.
NATIVE HABITAT: Eastern Asia.
SPECIAL CHARACTERISTICS: All parts are poisonous making it extremely deer resistant.

Arabis caucasica
ROCK-CRESS

DEER ATTRACTION: Rarely.
HABIT: Low and spreading often forming mats.
SIZE: 6–10" tall, spreads 18" or more.
LEAVES: 1–3" wide, with a fine white-gray fuzz.
FLOWERS: Fragrant white, no more than 1/2" wide, appear in early spring.
TEXTURE: Fine.
CULTURE: Full sun. Prefers moist, well drained soils, but will tolerate dry conditions.
LANDSCAPE/ GARDEN VALUE: Good for edging borders or beds. Use in rock and wall gardens.
HARDINESS: Zone 3.
NATIVE HABITAT: Europe (Caucasus area).
SPECIAL CHARACTERISTICS: Variegated leaved and double pink and white flowering varieties are available.

Artemisia schmidtiana
WORMWOOD

DEER ATTRACTION: Rarely.
HABIT: Low and spreading, often forming mounds.
SIZE: 1 2' tall, 18" or more wide.
LEAVES: Silvery gray, deeply cut leaves are covered with a very fine fuzz.
FLOWERS: Inconspicuous.
TEXTURE: Very fine.
CULTURE: Full sun and moist, liking well drained to poor, dry soils. Cut back hard in late summer to rejuvenate foliage growth.
LANDSCAPE/ GARDEN VALUE: Use as edging or ground cover.
HARDINESS: Zone 2.
SPECIAL CHARACTERISTICS: Over the years it forms mounds that tend to thin out in the middle and therefore needs to be dug up, divided, and replanted every few years.

Asclepias tuberosa

BUTTERFLY MILKWEED

DEER ATTRACTION: Rarely.
HABIT: Upright.
SIZE: 3' tall, 18" wide.
LEAVES: 2–6" long and lance-like, green covered with short, stiff
 hairs.
FLOWERS: 1/3" wide, orange, appear in showy clusters above plant
 in August and September.
TEXTURE: Medium.
CULTURE: Full sun. Does well in dry, sandy soils.
LANDSCAPE/ GARDEN VALUE: A popular flowering perennial. Use in
 sunny perennial and mixed borders. Great for use on banks and
 berms where soils may tend to dry quickly. A native wild-
 flower.
HARDINESS: Zone 3.
NATIVE HABITAT: Meadows of Eastern United States from
 Maine to Florida.
SPECIAL CHARACTERISTICS: Flowers attract butterflies and make good
 long lasting cut flowers.

Aster novi-belgi

NEW YORK ASTERS

DEER ATTRACTION: Rarely.
HABIT: Upright.
SIZE: 3–5' tall, 18" wide, although there are numerous smaller and compact cultivars.
LEAVES: 6–7" long, narrowly pointed, deep green.
FLOWERS: 1–3" wide, white, pink, blue to violet, with yellow centers. Blooms from early
 September until frost.
TEXTURE: Fine.
CULTURE: Full sun to light shade. Prefers rich, moist, well drained soils. Does best when
 summers are cool and moist. Many taller growing cultivars may need to be staked.
 Dig and divide clumps every few years to keep plants vigorous.
LANDSCAPE/ GARDEN VALUE: Great for late summer and autumn color in perennial and
 mixed flower borders. Use taller varieties as background plants, shorter growing types
 in front or at edges. The smallest varieties are great for use in rock gardens.
HARDINESS: Zone 2–3.   **NATIVE HABITAT:** Eastern North America.
SPECIAL CHARACTERISTICS: Great for fall color. Numerous cultivars of various flower colors
 and plant sizes are available. Suitable for use as a cut flower.

PERENNIALS

Astilbe x arendsii
HYBRID ASTILBE

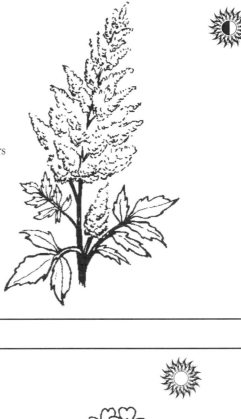

DEER ATTRACTION: Rarely.
HABIT: Upright.
SIZE: 2–4' tall, 2 -3' wide. Sizes vary according to cultivar.
LEAVES: 6–18" long, compound, green although some cultivars have
    bronze leaves.
FLOWERS: Very small, appearing on 6–12" upright feathery spikes, in
    shades of white, light pink to deep red and lavender. Blooming occurs
    from late May to August, depending on cultivar.
TEXTURE: Fine.
CULTURE: Prefers partial shade. Likes cool, moist, rich, well drained soil.
    Can be grown in full sun but need adequate moisture levels main-
    tained to avoid leaf scorching and reduced vigor.
LANDSCAPE/ GARDEN VALUE: A popular flowering perennial for shade.
    Use in shady perennial and mixed beds and borders.
HARDINESS: Zones 5–8.
NATIVE HABITAT: These hybrids come from Germany.
SPECIAL CHARACTERISTICS: Over 30 cultivars are available.

Aubretia deltoidea
PURPLE ROCK-CRESS

DEER ATTRACTION: Rarely.
HABIT: Low and spreading, often forming mats.
SIZE: 6–8" high, spreading to 18" or more.
LEAVES: 1" long gray-green, oval to spoon shaped with serrated edges,
    covered with tiny hairs.
FLOWERS: 3/4" wide with four petals. Comes in shades of mostly blue,
    but purples and reds are also common. Blooms April through
    June.
TEXTURE: Fine.
CULTURE: Full sun. Prefers poor, well drained, rocky soils. Does best in
    cooler climates. Cut back hard after first bloom when flowers fade
    to keep growth compact and encourage secondary bloom.
LANDSCAPE/ GARDEN VALUE: Use as edging in sunny beds and borders.
    Great for use in rock gardens and in crevices of rock walls.
HARDINESS: Zone 5–7.
NATIVE HABITAT: Europe and Asia Minor.

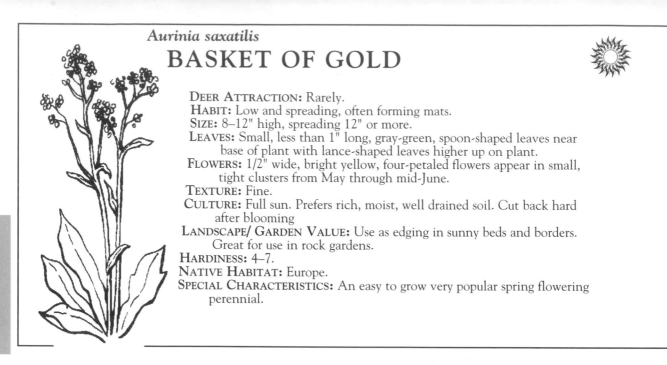

Aurinia saxatilis

BASKET OF GOLD

DEER ATTRACTION: Rarely.
HABIT: Low and spreading, often forming mats.
SIZE: 8–12" high, spreading 12" or more.
LEAVES: Small, less than 1" long, gray-green, spoon-shaped leaves near base of plant with lance-shaped leaves higher up on plant.
FLOWERS: 1/2" wide, bright yellow, four-petaled flowers appear in small, tight clusters from May through mid-June.
TEXTURE: Fine.
CULTURE: Full sun. Prefers rich, moist, well drained soil. Cut back hard after blooming
LANDSCAPE/ GARDEN VALUE: Use as edging in sunny beds and borders. Great for use in rock gardens.
HARDINESS: 4–7.
NATIVE HABITAT: Europe.
SPECIAL CHARACTERISTICS: An easy to grow very popular spring flowering perennial.

Coreopsis lanceolata

LANCE COREOPSIS

DEER ATTRACTION: Rarely.
HABIT: Upright.
SIZE: 2' tall, 18" wide.
LEAVES: 1 1/2–2" long, lance-like, green, and borne on lower half of the plant.
FLOWERS: 2 1/2" across, yellow, appear throughout the summer.
TEXTURE: Fine.
CULTURE: Full sun. Does well in almost any garden soil. Prefers dry, light soils. Constantly remove faded flowers to encourage new ones.
LANDSCAPE/ GARDEN VALUE: Use in sunny perennial and mixed beds and borders. Great for rock gardens and wildflower gardens.
HARDINESS: Zone 3–9.
NATIVE HABITAT: Eastern North America.
SPECIAL CHARACTERISTICS: A native wildflower.

Delphinium elatum

LARKSPUR

DEER ATTRACTION: Rarely.
HABIT: Upright.
SIZE: 4–6' tall, 2" wide.
LEAVES: 3–5" palmate, serrated edges, green.
FLOWERS: 1–2" wide, blue or purple, single or double flowers. Blooms appear in June and July. Hybrids offer more color variations of blue, violet, purple, pink, and white.
TEXTURE: Coarse.
CULTURE: Full sun. Grows best in rich, moist, well drained and slightly alkaline soils. Prefers cool, moist summers. Plant in areas protected from wind or provide sturdy stakes. Flower stalks are especially brittle and need staking. Responds well to heavy feeding. Constantly remove faded flowers to encourage new ones.
LANDSCAPE/ GARDEN VALUE: Use as a background plant in perennial beds and borders.
HARDINESS: Zone 2–9.
NATIVE HABITAT: Siberia.
SPECIAL CHARACTERISTICS: Considered a short-lived perennial, many treat *Delphiniums* as an annual or biennial. Suitable for use as a cut flower.

Echinacea purpurea

PURPLE CONEFLOWER

DEER ATTRACTION: Rarely.
HABIT: Upright.
SIZE: 2–4' tall, spreads to 18" or more.
LEAVES: 2–3" long, lance-shaped, green with serrated edges.
FLOWERS: 2 1/2–3" wide, purple or white daisy-like flowers that appear in July and August.
TEXTURE: Coarse.
CULTURE: Full sun. Does well in almost any well drained fertile soil.
LANDSCAPE/ GARDEN VALUE: Use in sunny perennial or mixed beds and borders or wildflower gardens.
HARDINESS: Zones 3–9.
NATIVE HABITAT: North America.
SPECIAL CHARACTERISTICS: A native North American wildflower. Suitable for use as a cut flower.

Filipendula ulmaria
MEADOWSWEET

DEER ATTRACTION: Rarely.
HABIT: Upright.
SIZE: 3–6' tall, 1–2' spread.
LEAVES: Large, 3–4" long, 3–5 lobed and deeply serrated leaflets, dark-green with white hairs beneath.
FLOWERS: 2–3" wide clusters of fragrant, creamy white flowers appear in July and August.
TEXTURE: Coarse.
CULTURE: Full sun or partial shade. Like rich, moist, well drained soils. Will do well in wet soils.
LANDSCAPE/ GARDEN VALUE: Good for use in lightly shaded perennial beds and borders and in between shrubs in wet areas. Also good for use in boggy areas.
HARDINESS: Zones 3–9.
NATIVE HABITAT: Europe and Asia.

Geranium
CRANESBILL

DEER ATTRACTION: Rarely.
HABIT: This group of plants is comprised of members (over 400 species) that exhibit various habits from low and spreading to upright.
SIZE: 6–36" tall, 8–36" spread.
LEAVES: Small, many lobes, and green.
FLOWERS: 1/2–2" across with 5 petals. Colors range from white, pink, blue, to purple. Bloom time varies among species, late spring, summer and fall.
TEXTURE: Fine.
CULTURE: Full sun. Adapts to almost any well drained soil. Cut back hard after first flowers fade to encourage more. Taller species may need staking. Dig and divide every 3–4 years to rejuvenate. Most are very insect and disease free.
LANDSCAPE/ GARDEN VALUE: Use as goundcovers, in perennial beds and borders and as accent plants around shrubs. A large group that contains many species are useful in various situations.
HARDINESS: Zone 4–8 depending on specie.
NATIVE HABITAT: North America, Asia, and Europe.

Helenium autumnale
SNEEZEWEED

DEER ATTRACTION: Rarely.
HABIT: Upright, forming a clump.
SIZE: 3–6' tall, 2–3' wide.
LEAVES: 5–6" long, lance-like with serrated edge, and green. Leaves extend down and along stem giving stem a winged look.
FLOWERS: 2" wide, yellow, drooping, almost daisy-like flower with terminal end of petals notched. Blooms in August through October.
TEXTURE: Medium.
CULTURE: Full sun. Adapts to almost any well drained soil. Often needs staking. Dig and divide every 3 years to rejuvenate clumps.
LANDSCAPE/ GARDEN VALUE: Use in perennial beds and borders and wildflower gardens.
HARDINESS: Zone 3–8.
NATIVE HABITAT: Eastern North America.
SPECIAL CHARACTERISTICS: Suitable for use as a cut flower.

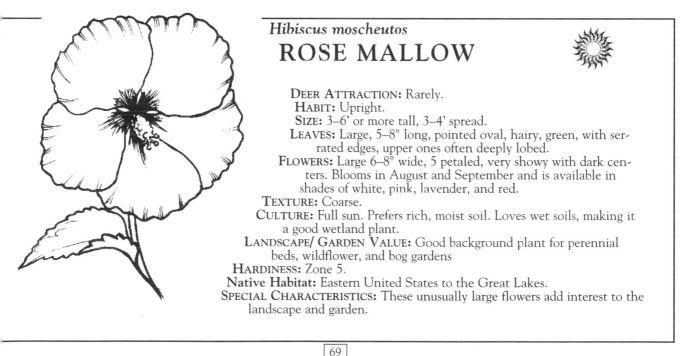

Hibiscus moscheutos
ROSE MALLOW

DEER ATTRACTION: Rarely.
HABIT: Upright.
SIZE: 3–6' or more tall, 3–4' spread.
LEAVES: Large, 5–8" long, pointed oval, hairy, green, with serrated edges, upper ones often deeply lobed.
FLOWERS: Large 6–8" wide, 5 petaled, very showy with dark centers. Blooms in August and September and is available in shades of white, pink, lavender, and red.
TEXTURE: Coarse.
CULTURE: Full sun. Prefers rich, moist soil. Loves wet soils, making it a good wetland plant.
LANDSCAPE/ GARDEN VALUE: Good background plant for perennial beds, wildflower, and bog gardens
HARDINESS: Zone 5.
NATIVE HABITAT: Eastern United States to the Great Lakes.
SPECIAL CHARACTERISTICS: These unusually large flowers add interest to the landscape and garden.

Lychnis coronaria

ROSE CAMPION

DEER ATTRACTION: Rarely.
HABIT: Upright.
SIZE: 2–3' tall, 18" wide.
LEAVES: 4" long, oval covered with gray woolly fuzz giving the plant a silvery appearance.
FLOWERS: 1" wide, bright crimson, red–pink flowers appear in clusters in June and July.
TEXTURE: Medium.
CULTURE: Full sun to partial shade. Likes almost any well drained soil.
LANDSCAPE/ GARDEN VALUE: Use in perennial beds and borders.
HARDINESS: Zones 4–8.
NATIVE HABITAT: Southern Europe.
SPECIAL CHARACTERISTICS: Silvery foliage provides good contrast and lightens shaded areas.

Lysimachia clethroides

JAPANESE LOOSESTRIFE

DEER ATTRACTION: Rarely.
HABIT: Upright.
SIZE: 2–3' tall and wide.
LEAVES: 3–6" long lance-shaped, gray-green.
FLOWERS: 1/2" wide, white, appear on dense, 6–8" long, curved spikes.
TEXTURE: Coarse.
CULTURE: Full sun or partial shade. Prefers moist soils. Remove faded flowers to prevent it from seeding itself.
LANDSCAPE/ GARDEN VALUE: Mostly used in perennial borders and bog gardens.
HARDINESS: Zone 3–8.
NATIVE HABITAT: Japan and China.
SPECIAL CHARACTERISTICS: Can become invasive if neglected.

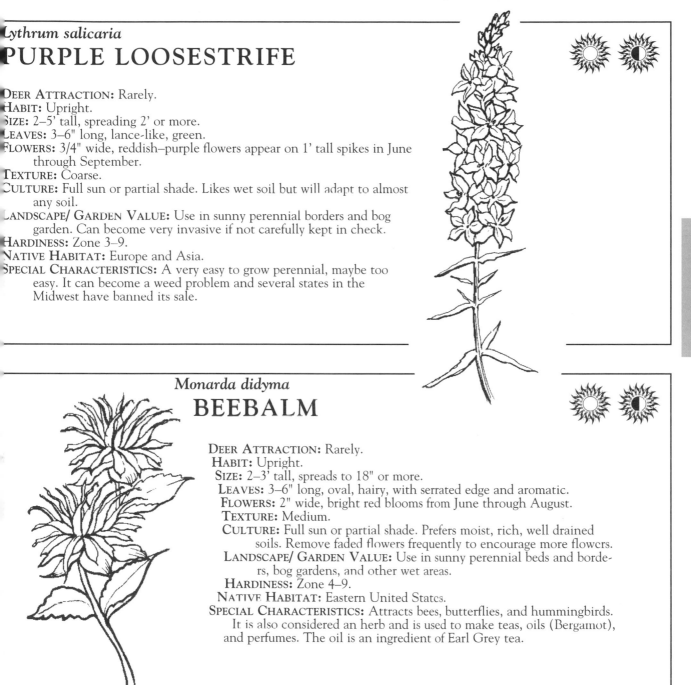

Lythrum salicaria
PURPLE LOOSESTRIFE

DEER ATTRACTION: Rarely.
HABIT: Upright.
SIZE: 2–5' tall, spreading 2' or more.
LEAVES: 3–6" long, lance-like, green.
FLOWERS: 3/4" wide, reddish–purple flowers appear on 1' tall spikes in June through September.
TEXTURE: Coarse.
CULTURE: Full sun or partial shade. Likes wet soil but will adapt to almost any soil.
LANDSCAPE/ GARDEN VALUE: Use in sunny perennial borders and bog garden. Can become very invasive if not carefully kept in check.
HARDINESS: Zone 3–9.
NATIVE HABITAT: Europe and Asia.
SPECIAL CHARACTERISTICS: A very easy to grow perennial, maybe too easy. It can become a weed problem and several states in the Midwest have banned its sale.

Monarda didyma
BEEBALM

DEER ATTRACTION: Rarely.
HABIT: Upright.
SIZE: 2–3' tall, spreads to 18" or more.
LEAVES: 3–6" long, oval, hairy, with serrated edge and aromatic.
FLOWERS: 2" wide, bright red blooms from June through August.
TEXTURE: Medium.
CULTURE: Full sun or partial shade. Prefers moist, rich, well drained soils. Remove faded flowers frequently to encourage more flowers.
LANDSCAPE/ GARDEN VALUE: Use in sunny perennial beds and borders, bog gardens, and other wet areas.
HARDINESS: Zone 4–9.
NATIVE HABITAT: Eastern United States.
SPECIAL CHARACTERISTICS: Attracts bees, butterflies, and hummingbirds. It is also considered an herb and is used to make teas, oils (Bergamot), and perfumes. The oil is an ingredient of Earl Grey tea.

Paeonia officinalis

COMMON PEONY

DEER ATTRACTION: Rarely.
HABIT: Upright.
SIZE: 3' tall and wide.
LEAVES: 12" or more long, consisting of two groups of three 4–6"
leaflets. Bonze buds emerge from ground in spring, turning to
green, leathery leaves.
FLOWERS: 4" across, ranging from deep red, pink, to shades of white.
Flowers are available in single or double forms and appear in
late May.
TEXTURE: Medium.
CULTURE: Full sun. Prefers well prepared soils that are moist, well
drained and enriched with compost or well rotted cow manure.
Care should be taken when planting to make sure crowns
(where buds emerge) are no deeper than 2" or plants may fail
to bloom. Peonies respond well to a side-dressing of well rotted cow manure in early spring and after blooming.
LANDSCAPE/ GARDEN VALUE: An old-fashioned favorite. Makes an excellent choice for a sunny mixed border.

Perovskia x hybrida

RUSSIAN SAGE

DEER ATTRACTION: Rarely.
HABIT: Upright, very shrublike.
SIZE: 3–4' tall, spreading to over 3'.
LEAVES: 2–3" long, lance-like, that can be variably cut and toothed and finely
divided, green-gray in color.
FLOWERS: Small purplish-blue, appear on 3–6" loose and hairy spikes that
appear in mid to late summer.
TEXTURE: Fine.
CULTURE: Full sun. Adapts to almost any well drained soil. Plants should be cut
back to several inches from the ground in early spring to encourage dense
growth and flowering.
LANDSCAPE/ GARDEN VALUE: Great for contrast in sunny perennial or mixed beds
and borders.
HARDINESS: Zones 5–9.
NATIVE HABITAT: Eastern Asia.
SPECIAL CHARACTERISTICS: Loose, hairy flowers, and its fine foliage give this shrublike plant a
smokey blue appearance that contrasts well with large, yellow or daisy-like flowers.

PERENNIALS

72

Polemonium caeruleum
JACOB'S LADDER

DEER ATTRACTION: Rarely.
HABIT: Upright.
SIZE: 15–24" tall, spreads to over 18".
LEAVES: 4–6" long leaves made up of as many as 20–27 pairs of small, evenly spaced 1/2–1" long leaflets.
FLOWERS: 1" wide, cup-like blue flowers appear in late May through July.
TEXTURE: Fine.
CULTURE: Prefers to grow in partial shade and rich soil. Remove faded flowers to encourage more blooms.
LANDSCAPE/ GARDEN VALUE: Use in partially shaded perennial and mixed beds and borders.
HARDINESS: Zones 3–8.
NATIVE HABITAT: Europe.
SPECIAL CHARACTERISTICS: The evenly spaced leaflets of the leaves look like the rungs of a ladder, therefore its common name, Jacob's Ladder.

Rudbeckia maxima
BLACK-EYED SUSAN

DEER ATTRACTION: Rarely.
HABIT: Upright.
SIZE: 5–6' tall, 2' wide.
LEAVES: Up to 12" long, oval to spoon shaped, hairy, grayish-green leaves with serrated edges.
FLOWERS: Up to 5–6" wide, daisy-like, consisting of drooping, yellow petals surrounding a brown center that appear in July and August.
TEXTURE: Coarse.
CULTURE: Full sun to partial shade. Adapts to any well drained soil. Remove dead flowers to encourage a second blooming later in summer. May need staking.
LANDSCAPE/ GARDEN VALUE: Use as a background plant in sunny perennial and mixed beds and borders. Also looks impressive standing alone in mass plantings. A native plant great for use in wildflower gardens.
HARDINESS: Zones 4–9.
NATIVE HABITAT: North America.

73

Solidago hybrids
GOLDENROD

DEER ATTRACTION: Rarely.
HABIT: Upright.
SIZE: 2–3' tall, 18–24" wide.
LEAVES: 4–6" long, lance-like, green.
FLOWERS: Small, yellow, 4–6" long, drooping or horizontally held spikes
appear in July through October.
TEXTURE: Coarse.
CULTURE: Full sun or light shade. Grows in almost any well drained soil.
LANDSCAPE/ GARDEN VALUE: Use in sunny or lightly shaded perennial
or mixed beds and borders.
HARDINESS: Zones 3–9.
NATIVE HABITAT: North America, Europe, Asia, and South America.
SPECIAL CHARACTERISTICS: Very easy to grow perennial. Many new
hybrids and cultivars are available.

Stachys byzantina
LAMB'S EARS

DEER ATTRACTION: Rarely.
HABIT: Low, forming mats.
SIZE: 12–18" tall, 12" wide.
LEAVES: Woolly, 4–6" long, oblong, toothed edge, gray-whitish
green.
FLOWERS: 6–8" long purple spikes, appear in late May through June.
TEXTURE: Medium.
CULTURE: Full sun to partial shade. Prefers well drained, somewhat
moist soils. Not tolerant of dry soils.
LANDSCAPE/ GARDEN VALUE: Use as an edging plant in perennial
and mixed beds and borders. Also use as a ground cover.
HARDINESS: Zones 4–8.
NATIVE HABITAT: Turkey and Southwestern Asia.
SPECIAL CHARACTERISTICS: Can sometimes look messy as
stems flop over and lay prostrate later in season.

Thymus vulgaris
COMMON THYME

DEER ATTRACTION: Rarely.
HABIT: Very low and spreading.
SIZE: Up to 2" high.
LEAVES: Evergreen, 1/2" long, dark green and very aromatic.
FLOWERS: Small lilac or purple, fragrant, appear on short upright spikes in May.
TEXTURE: Very fine.
CULTURE: Full sun to partial shade. Will adapt to almost any well drained soil.
LANDSCAPE/ GARDEN VALUE: Use in rock gardens or edges of borders. Can be planted and grown between stepping stones and in the cracks and crevices of rock walls.
HARDINESS: Zone 6.
NATIVE HABITAT: Southern Europe.
SPECIAL CHARACTERISTICS: Often used as an herb for flavoring foods.

Tiarella cordifolia
FOAMFLOWER

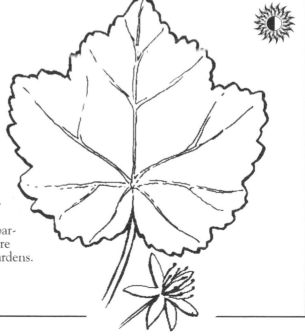

DEER ATTRACTION: Rarely.
HABIT: Low and spreading.
SIZE: 6–12" tall, spreading 18" or more.
LEAVES: Evergreen (in mild climates), 4" wide, heart-shaped with 5–7 lobes, light green and hairy.
FLOWERS: 3–4" long upright spikes covered with small, delicate white flowers. Blooming occurs in April though July.
TEXTURE: Medium.
CULTURE: Prefers partial shade. Does best in organically rich, moist but well drained soil. Will usually spread rapidly if provided with adequate moisture throughout summer.
LANDSCAPE/ GARDEN VALUE: One of the best ground covers for partial shade. Use in perennial and mixed beds and borders where lightly shaded conditions exist. Great for native woodland gardens.
HARDINESS: Zones 3–8.
NATIVE HABITAT: Eastern North America.

Yucca filamentosa

ADAM'S NEEDLE

DEER ATTRACTION: Rarely.
HABIT: Large upright spiked clump.
SIZE: 3–4' tall and wide.
LEAVES: Evergreen, 2 1/2–3' long, 1–2" wide, lance-shaped, stiff and green.
FLOWERS: 2–3" wide, hanging, creamy-white flowers appear on 1–3' tall spikes in July.
TEXTURE: Very coarse.
CULTURE: Full sun. Does best in rich, moist, well drained soils, but is extremely tolerant of hot, dry areas.
LANDSCAPE/ GARDEN VALUE: Use as specimen or focal point in landscapes beds and borders.
HARDINESS: Zone 4.
NATIVE HABITAT: Eastern United States, Mid–Atlantic, southwest to Mexico.
SPECIAL CHARACTERISTICS: Very unique looking, provides a desert or southwest look. Very deer resistant.

Ageratum houstonianum
AGERATUM OR FLOSSFLOWER

DEER ATTRACTION: Seldomly.
HABIT: Low and spreading.
SIZE: 6–18" tall, 12–24" wide.
LEAVES: 1 1/2–3" wide, rounded, heart-shaped, green.
FLOWERS: 1–2" puffy clusters of small blue, white, or pink flowers that cover the entire top of plant.
TEXTURE: Medium.
CULTURE: Full sun to partial shade. Prefers rich, moist, well drained soil with a neutral pH.
LANDSCAPE/ GARDEN VALUE: Use as edging in annual or mixed beds and borders. Good for containers.
HARDINESS: Not frost tolerant.
NATIVE HABITAT: Mexico.
SPECIAL CHARACTERISTICS: Several dwarf varieties are available that grow to no more than 2–4" tall.

Antirrhinum majus
SNAPDRAGON

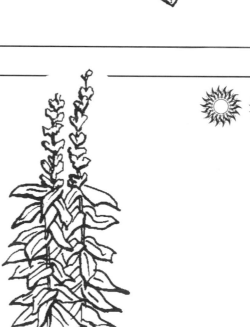

DEER ATTRACTION: Rarely.
HABIT: Upright.
SIZE: 6–36" tall, 10–18" wide.
LEAVES: 3" long, lance-like, green.
FLOWERS: 1 1/2" long, white, pink, red, yellow or orange, appear on 8–12" spikes.
TEXTURE: Medium.
CULTURE: Full sun or partial shade. Prefers rich, moist, well drained soil with a neutral pH.
LANDSCAPE/ GARDEN VALUE: Use in annual and mixed beds and borders.
HARDINESS: Not frost tolerant.
NATIVE HABITAT: Mediterranean region of Europe.

ANNUALS

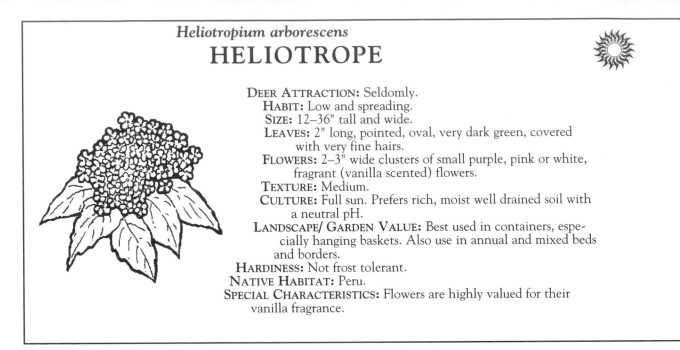

Heliotropium arborescens
HELIOTROPE

DEER ATTRACTION: Seldomly.
HABIT: Low and spreading.
SIZE: 12–36" tall and wide.
LEAVES: 2" long, pointed, oval, very dark green, covered with very fine hairs.
FLOWERS: 2–3" wide clusters of small purple, pink or white, fragrant (vanilla scented) flowers.
TEXTURE: Medium.
CULTURE: Full sun. Prefers rich, moist well drained soil with a neutral pH.
LANDSCAPE/ GARDEN VALUE: Best used in containers, especially hanging baskets. Also use in annual and mixed beds and borders.
HARDINESS: Not frost tolerant.
NATIVE HABITAT: Peru.
SPECIAL CHARACTERISTICS: Flowers are highly valued for their vanilla fragrance.

Ipomoea alba
MOONFLOWER

DEER ATTRACTION: Rarely.
HABIT: Trailing vine.
SIZE: 15' or more.
LEAVES: 2–3" heart-shaped, green.
FLOWERS: 1 1/2–2" wide, white fragrant flowers that open at night.
TEXTURE: Medium.
CULTURE: Full sun. Prefers rich, moist, well drained soil with a neutral pH, but will tolerate dry infertile soils.
LANDSCAPE/ GARDEN VALUE: Use to cover trellis, fences or walls.
HARDINESS: Not frost tolerant.
SPECIAL CHARACTERISTICS: Fragrant night bloomer.

ANNUALS

Ipomoea purpurea
MORNING GLORY

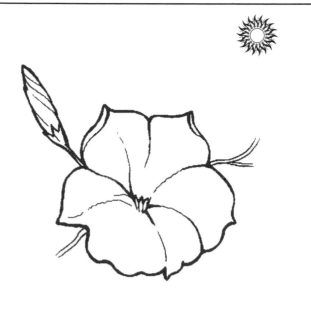

DEER ATTRACTION: Rarely.
HABIT: Twining vine.
SIZE: 15' or more.
LEAVES: 2–3" heart-shaped, green.
FLOWERS: 2–3" wide, trumpet-shaped, come in red, white or purple.
TEXTURE: Medium.
CULTURE: Full sun. Prefers rich, moist well drained soil with a neutral pH.
LANDSCAPE/ GARDEN VALUE: Use to cover trellis, fences or walls.
HARDINESS: Not frost tolerant.
SPECIAL CHARACTERISTICS: Morning Glory can become invasive and is considered a weed in many east coast states.

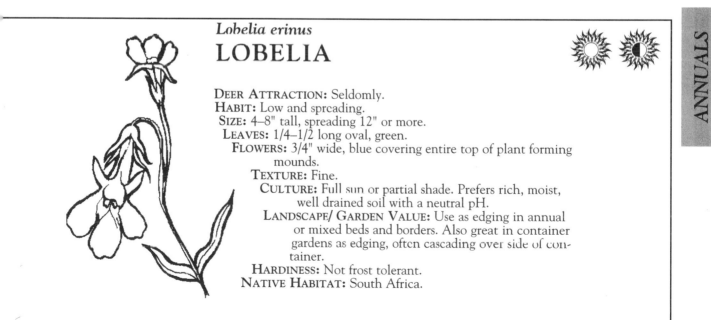

Lobelia erinus
LOBELIA

DEER ATTRACTION: Seldomly.
HABIT: Low and spreading.
SIZE: 4–8" tall, spreading 12" or more.
LEAVES: 1/4–1/2 long oval, green.
FLOWERS: 3/4" wide, blue covering entire top of plant forming mounds.
TEXTURE: Fine.
CULTURE: Full sun or partial shade. Prefers rich, moist, well drained soil with a neutral pH.
LANDSCAPE/ GARDEN VALUE: Use as edging in annual or mixed beds and borders. Also great in container gardens as edging, often cascading over side of container.
HARDINESS: Not frost tolerant.
NATIVE HABITAT: South Africa.

Mimulus cupreus
MONKEY FLOWER

DEER ATTRACTION: Seldomly.
HABIT: Upright and spreading.
SIZE: 8" tall and wide.
LEAVES: 1 1/4" long, elongated, oval, green.
FLOWERS: 1 1/2" long, tubular yellow flowers with 2 lips and spreading lobes that turn orange-brown. June and July is the peak bloom time.
TEXTURE: Medium.
CULTURE: Prefers shaded location. Adapts to any rich, moist, well drained soil.
LANDSCAPE/ GARDEN VALUE: Use in shady annual and mixed beds and borders, especially effective when used as edging, in front of taller plants.
HARDINESS: Not frost tolerant.
NATIVE HABITAT: Chile.
SPECIAL CHARACTERISTICS: Great choice for shady areas.

Mirabilis jalapa
FOUR O'CLOCKS

DEER ATTRACTION: Seldomly.
HABIT: Upright.
SIZE: 24–36" tall, 18–24" wide.
LEAVES: 2–2 1/2" long, elongated, heart-like, dark green.
FLOWERS: 1–2" wide, funnel-shaped, white, yellow or red. Flowers open about 4 o'clock in the afternoon. Blooms freely throughout the summer.
TEXTURE: Medium.
CULTURE: Full sun. Prefer light, well drained soil.
LANDSCAPE/ GARDEN VALUE: Use in annual and mixed beds and borders.
HARDINESS: Not frost tolerant.
NATIVE HABITAT: Tropical regions of North and South America.
SPECIAL CHARACTERISTICS: Flowers open after about 4 o'clock in the afternoon, a concern if garden or landscape is usually viewed earlier in the day.

Petunia x hybrida
GARDEN PETUNIA

DEER ATTRACTION: Seldomly.
HABIT: Upright and prostrate varieties are available.
SIZE: 6–36" tall and wide.
LEAVES: 1–3" long, pointed, oval, green covered with fine hairs.
FLOWERS: 1–5" wide (varies according to variety), funnel shaped. Many colors available including white, red, purple, violet, and multi colored. Also available in ruffled and double flowering forms. Many hybrids available. Prime blooming time is from June until frost.
TEXTURE: Medium.
CULTURE: Full sun. Does best in rich, well drained soil. Plants may need to be cut back periodically when flowering begins to slow. Pinch back and fertilize to stimulate new blooms.
LANDSCAPE/ GARDEN VALUE: Use in annual and mixed beds and borders. Also great in containers and window boxes.
HARDINESS: Not frost tolerant.
NATIVE HABITAT: Argentina.
SPECIAL CHARACTERISTICS: The availability of many hybrids provides for a great selection of colors, flower, and plant types.

Salvia splendens
SCARLET SAGE

DEER ATTRACTION: Seldomly.
HABIT: Upright.
SIZE: 6–36" tall and wide.
LEAVES: 2 1/2–3 1/2" long, pointed, oval, dark green.
FLOWERS: 6–10" long, spike of small red, pink, purple, or white flowers.
TEXTURE: Medium.
CULTURE: Full sun to light shade. Prefers rich, moist, well drained soils.
LANDSCAPE/ GARDEN VALUE: Use in annual and mixed beds and borders. Also great in containers and window boxes.
HARDINESS: Not frost tolerant.
NATIVE HABITAT: Brazil.
SPECIAL CHARACTERISTICS: Many new hybrids are available.

ANNUALS

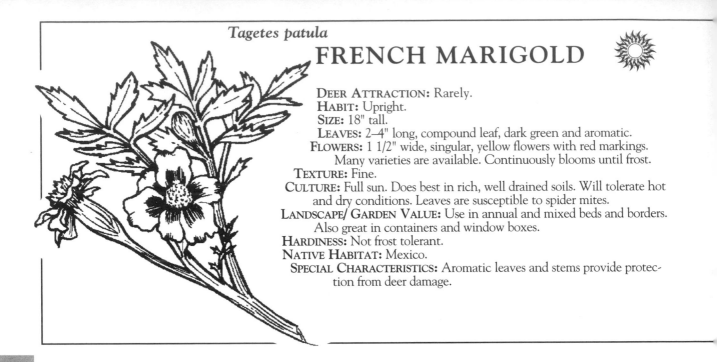

Tagetes patula

FRENCH MARIGOLD

DEER ATTRACTION: Rarely.
HABIT: Upright.
SIZE: 18" tall.
LEAVES: 2–4" long, compound leaf, dark green and aromatic.
FLOWERS: 1 1/2" wide, singular, yellow flowers with red markings. Many varieties are available. Continuously blooms until frost.
TEXTURE: Fine.
CULTURE: Full sun. Does best in rich, well drained soils. Will tolerate hot and dry conditions. Leaves are susceptible to spider mites.
LANDSCAPE/ GARDEN VALUE: Use in annual and mixed beds and borders. Also great in containers and window boxes.
HARDINESS: Not frost tolerant.
NATIVE HABITAT: Mexico.
SPECIAL CHARACTERISTICS: Aromatic leaves and stems provide protection from deer damage.

Tropaeolum majus

NASTURTIUM

DEER ATTRACTION: Rarely.
HABIT: Low and vine-types are available.
SIZE: 12–48" tall, some varieties can spread over 48".
LEAVES: 2" wide, round, light green.
FLOWERS: 2 1/2" wide, funnel-shaped flowers that come in variations of yellow, orange, and red. Single and double flowering varieties are available. Some varieties are very fragrant.
TEXTURE: Medium.
CULTURE: Full sun. Prefers rich, moist, well drained soil. Susceptible to aphids.
LANDSCAPE/ GARDEN VALUE: Use in annual and mixed beds and borders. Also use in containers, especially in hanging baskets and window boxes.
HARDINESS: Not frost tolerant.
NATIVE HABITAT: South and Central America.
SPECIAL CHARACTERISTICS: Leaves and stems have a bitter taste, making it resistant to deer damage.

ANNUALS

82

Allium giganteum
GIANT ORNAMENTAL ONION

DEER ATTRACTION: Rarely.
HABIT: Arching.
SIZE: 4' tall and wide.
LEAVES: 18–24" long, 2" wide. Shiny, dark green.
FLOWERS: Large, 4–5" wide ball of bright, blue flowers appear on 5' tall stalks in June.
TEXTURE: Coarse.
CULTURE: Full sun. Adapts to almost any moist, well drained soil.
LANDSCAPE/ GARDEN VALUE: Large flowers provide bold interest. Use in a group of 3–5 plants as a focal point in perennial or mixed beds and borders. Also great for accenting shrub beds and mass plantings.
HARDINESS: Zone 5.
NATIVE HABITAT: China.
SPECIAL CHARACTERISTICS: A very unique, colorful, and bold addition to any landscape or garden. Bulbs and plants give off a slightly unpleasant odor.

Fritillaria imperialis
CROWN IMPERIAL

DEER ATTRACTION: Rarely.
HABIT: Upright.
SIZE: 3' tall, 12–18" wide.
LEAVES: 8–10" long, 1" wide, lance-like and green, covering lower half of main stalk.
FLOWERS: 8–10 brilliant, 2" long, yellow or red hanging, bell-shaped flowers encircle the top of a 3' stalk that is crowned with a mound of 4–6" long leaves in April.
TEXTURE: Coarse.
CULTURE: Full sun. Does best in rich, moist, well drained soil. Clumps of bulbs benefit from being dug up and divided every 2–3 years.
LANDSCAPE/ GARDEN VALUE: Striking large flowers provide interest. Best used in groups of 3–5 plants as a focal point in perennial or mixed beds and borders. Also great for accenting shrub beds and mass plantings.
HARDINESS: Zone 5.
NATIVE HABITAT: Turkey, Iraq, and Iran.
SPECIAL CHARACTERISTICS: Bulbs and plant gives off a distinct and unpleasant

BULBS

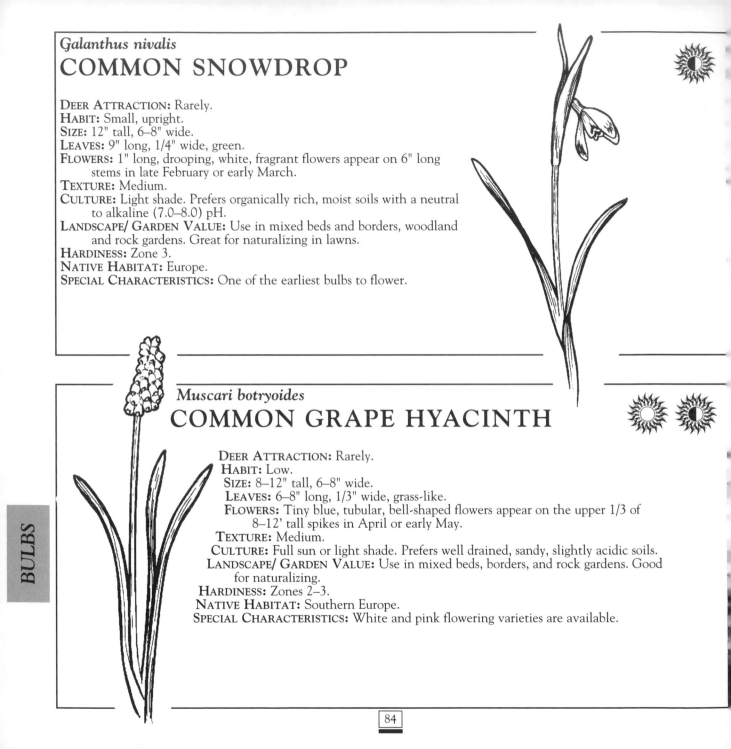

Galanthus nivalis
COMMON SNOWDROP

DEER ATTRACTION: Rarely.
HABIT: Small, upright.
SIZE: 12" tall, 6–8" wide.
LEAVES: 9" long, 1/4" wide, green.
FLOWERS: 1" long, drooping, white, fragrant flowers appear on 6" long stems in late February or early March.
TEXTURE: Medium.
CULTURE: Light shade. Prefers organically rich, moist soils with a neutral to alkaline (7.0–8.0) pH.
LANDSCAPE/ GARDEN VALUE: Use in mixed beds and borders, woodland and rock gardens. Great for naturalizing in lawns.
HARDINESS: Zone 3.
NATIVE HABITAT: Europe.
SPECIAL CHARACTERISTICS: One of the earliest bulbs to flower.

Muscari botryoides
COMMON GRAPE HYACINTH

DEER ATTRACTION: Rarely.
HABIT: Low.
SIZE: 8–12" tall, 6–8" wide.
LEAVES: 6–8" long, 1/3" wide, grass-like.
FLOWERS: Tiny blue, tubular, bell-shaped flowers appear on the upper 1/3 of 8–12' tall spikes in April or early May.
TEXTURE: Medium.
CULTURE: Full sun or light shade. Prefers well drained, sandy, slightly acidic soils.
LANDSCAPE/ GARDEN VALUE: Use in mixed beds, borders, and rock gardens. Good for naturalizing.
HARDINESS: Zones 2–3.
NATIVE HABITAT: Southern Europe.
SPECIAL CHARACTERISTICS: White and pink flowering varieties are available.

BULBS

84

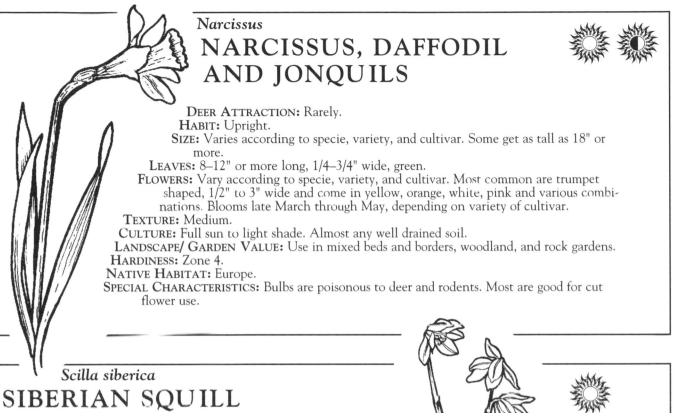

Narcissus
NARCISSUS, DAFFODIL AND JONQUILS

DEER ATTRACTION: Rarely.
HABIT: Upright.
SIZE: Varies according to specie, variety, and cultivar. Some get as tall as 18" or more.
LEAVES: 8–12" or more long, 1/4–3/4" wide, green.
FLOWERS: Vary according to specie, variety, and cultivar. Most common are trumpet shaped, 1/2" to 3" wide and come in yellow, orange, white, pink and various combinations. Blooms late March through May, depending on variety of cultivar.
TEXTURE: Medium.
CULTURE: Full sun to light shade. Almost any well drained soil.
LANDSCAPE/ GARDEN VALUE: Use in mixed beds and borders, woodland, and rock gardens.
HARDINESS: Zone 4.
NATIVE HABITAT: Europe.
SPECIAL CHARACTERISTICS: Bulbs are poisonous to deer and rodents. Most are good for cut flower use.

Scilla siberica
SIBERIAN SQUILL

DEER ATTRACTION: Rarely.
HABIT: Upright.
SIZE: 6" tall and wide.
LEAVES: 6" long, 3/4" wide, green.
FLOWERS: 1/2" wide, hanging deep blue flowers appear on 6" tall, upright stem in late March through April.
TEXTURE: Medium.
CULTURE: Full sun. Prefers organically rich, well drained, slightly acidic soil.
LANDSCAPE/ GARDEN VALUE: Use in mixed beds, borders, and rock gardens.
HARDINESS: Zones 2 -3.
NATIVE HABITAT: Siberia.
SPECIAL CHARACTERISTICS: A white, flowering variety is available.

BULKS

Allium shoenoprasum
CHIVES

DEER ATTRACTION: Rarely.
HABIT: Upright.
SIZE: 8–12" tall.
LEAVES: 6–10" long and tubular, dark green in color.
FLOWERS: Small, 1/2–3/4" wide, rosy-lavender in color appear in
June–September.
TEXTURE: Fine.
CULTURE: Full sun. Will adapt to almost any well drained soil.
Occasionally cut and harvest leaves which emerge from underground
bulblets.
LANDSCAPE/ GARDEN VALUE: Ornamentally used in rock gardens. An essential
in herb gardens. Makes a great potted herb.
HARDINESS: Zones 2–3.
NATIVE HABITAT: Europe and Asia.
SPECIAL CHARACTERISTICS: Mild, onion flavored leaves are used for flavoring sal-
ads and in cooking.

Angelica archangelica
ANGELICA

DEER ATTRACTION: Rarely.
HABIT: Very tall, upright growing herb.
SIZE: 5–8' tall, 3' tall.
LEAVES: 6–10" long, thrice compound, green, very fragrant leaves.
FLOWERS: Large, 4–6" wide clumps of smaller greenish-white flowers appear in late June
through early August.
TEXTURE: Coarse.
CULTURE: Full sun. Prefers rich, moist, well drained soils. Will tolerate dryer soils as
well.
LANDSCAPE/ GARDEN VALUE: Herb gardens. Limited ornamental value.
HARDINESS: Zone 4.
SPECIAL CHARACTERISTICS: Young leaves are used in cooking fish. Blanched stems
may be eaten like celery. Roots and stems are used to flavor liqueurs. Candied
leaves and stems are used to decorate cakes and other sweet foods. Medicinal
uses include treatments for indigestion, anemia, coughs, and colds.

Hyssopus officinalis
HYSSOP

DEER ATTRACTION: Rarely.
HABIT: Upright and shrubby.
SIZE: 1 1/2–2' tall and wide.
LEAVES: 1" long, green and aromatic.
FLOWERS: Tiny, blue flowers on 2 1/2–5" long upright spikes appear in July through September. Flowers attract butterflies and bees.
TEXTURE: Fine.
CULTURE: Full sun. Almost any well drained soil will do.
LANDSCAPE/ GARDEN VALUE: Herb gardens. Makes a great ground cover or low growing hedge. Also makes a great potted herb.
HARDINESS: Zones 2-3.
NATIVE HABITAT: Mediterranean.
SPECIAL CHARACTERISTICS: Medicinal uses include treatment for colds, flu, bronchitis, bruises, and burns.

Lavandula officinalis
LAVENDER

DEER ATTRACTION: Rarely.
HABIT: Upright.
SIZE: 3' tall, 2' wide.
LEAVES: 4–6" long, very narrow, gray-green and aromatic.
FLOWERS: 4–6" long, spikes of tiny, lavender colored, aromatic flowers that appear in June.
TEXTURE: Fine.
CULTURE: Full sun. Adapts well to almost any well drained soil and tolerates hot, dry conditions. Cut back to the ground in spring. After blooming, prune back to remove dead flowers and rejuvenate plant.
LANDSCAPE/ GARDEN VALUE: Great for use in perennial flower beds and borders as well as herb gardens. Can be pruned into a low hedge.
HARDINESS: Zone 5.
NATIVE HABITAT: Southern Europe and Africa.
SPECIAL CHARACTERISTICS: Dried flowers are are used to make fragrant sachets. Medicinal uses include treatment for burns, stings, headache, coughs, and colds.

HERBS

Marrubium vulgare
HOREHOUND

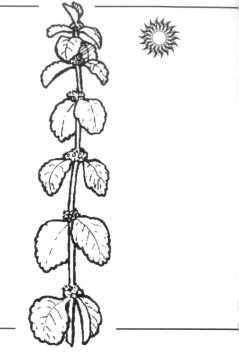

DEER ATTRACTION: Rarely.
HABIT: Upright.
SIZE: 3' tall, 2' wide.
LEAVES: 1 1/2–2" long, almost round with shallow and rounded serrated edges, gray-green in color; hairy. Aromatic.
FLOWERS: Small clusters of tiny, whitish flowers appear along stem where leaves emerge from stem (at axils) in June–August.
TEXTURE: Medium.
CULTURE: Full sun. Does best in well drained soils, tolerates dry soils.
LANDSCAPE/ GARDEN VALUE: Somewhat ornamental, use in herb gardens and perennial beds and borders.
HARDINESS: Zone 3.
NATIVE HABITAT: Europe.
SPECIAL CHARACTERISTICS: Leaves and stems are used to flavor candy and cough drops. Medicinal uses include treatment of respiratory and digestive disorders.

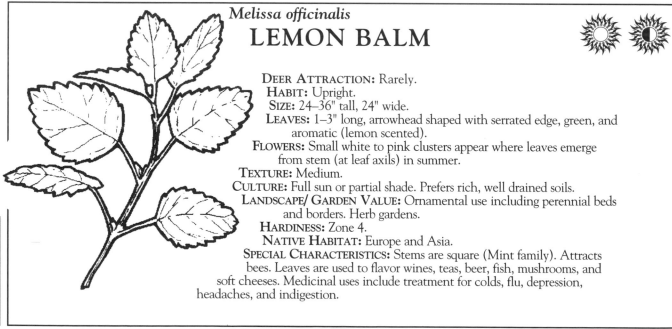

Melissa officinalis
LEMON BALM

DEER ATTRACTION: Rarely.
HABIT: Upright.
SIZE: 24–36" tall, 24" wide.
LEAVES: 1–3" long, arrowhead shaped with serrated edge, green, and aromatic (lemon scented).
FLOWERS: Small white to pink clusters appear where leaves emerge from stem (at leaf axils) in summer.
TEXTURE: Medium.
CULTURE: Full sun or partial shade. Prefers rich, well drained soils.
LANDSCAPE/ GARDEN VALUE: Ornamental use including perennial beds and borders. Herb gardens.
HARDINESS: Zone 4.
NATIVE HABITAT: Europe and Asia.
SPECIAL CHARACTERISTICS: Stems are square (Mint family). Attracts bees. Leaves are used to flavor wines, teas, beer, fish, mushrooms, and soft cheeses. Medicinal uses include treatment for colds, flu, depression, headaches, and indigestion.

HERBS

88

Mentha piperita
PEPPERMINT

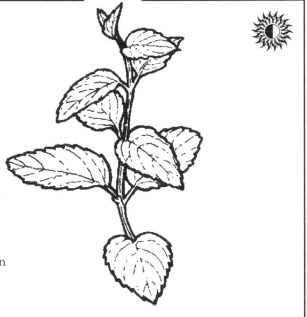

DEER ATTRACTION: Rarely.
HABIT: Upright.
SIZE: 1–3" tall, 2' wide.
LEAVES: 3" long, 1 1/2" wide, pointed, green, with strong aromatic peppermint odor. Square stems.
FLOWERS: 1–3" long, spikes covered with tiny, purple flowers in autumn.
TEXTURE: Medium.
CULTURE: Light shade. Prefers rich, moist, well drained soils.
LANDSCAPE/ GARDEN VALUE: Ornamental use including perennial beds, borders, and herb gardens.
HARDINESS: Zone 3.
NATIVE HABITAT: Europe.
SPECIAL CHARACTERISTICS: Widely used for flavoring foods especially sweets. Medicinal uses include treatment for indigestion and colds.

Mentha pulegium
EUROPEAN PENNYROYAL

DEER ATTRACTION: Rarely.
HABIT: Low and spreading.
SIZE: Up to 12" tall, spreads continuously.
LEAVES: 1/2" long, oval, green, with strong minty odor.
FLOWERS: Small blue flowers appear around stems at axils (where leaves emerge from stems).
TEXTURE: Fine.
CULTURE: Light shade. Prefers rich, moist, well drained soils.
LANDSCAPE/ GARDEN VALUE: Ornamental use including annual beds and borders, edging, or ground cover. Herb gardens.
HARDINESS: Zone 7.
NATIVE HABITAT: Europe and Asia.
SPECIAL CHARACTERISTICS: Not tolerant to extreme cold; use as an annual. Leaves are used to repel insects. Medicinal uses include treatment for colds and flu.

HERBS

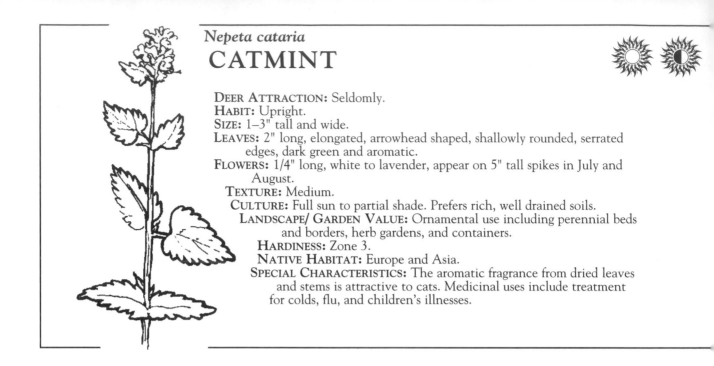

Nepeta cataria
CATMINT

DEER ATTRACTION: Seldomly.
HABIT: Upright.
SIZE: 1–3" tall and wide.
LEAVES: 2" long, elongated, arrowhead shaped, shallowly rounded, serrated edges, dark green and aromatic.
FLOWERS: 1/4" long, white to lavender, appear on 5" tall spikes in July and August.
TEXTURE: Medium.
CULTURE: Full sun to partial shade. Prefers rich, well drained soils.
LANDSCAPE/ GARDEN VALUE: Ornamental use including perennial beds and borders, herb gardens, and containers.
HARDINESS: Zone 3.
NATIVE HABITAT: Europe and Asia.
SPECIAL CHARACTERISTICS: The aromatic fragrance from dried leaves and stems is attractive to cats. Medicinal uses include treatment for colds, flu, and children's illnesses.

Ocimum basilicum
ORIGANUM VULGARE (BASIL)

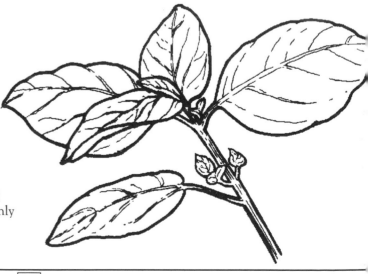

DEER ATTRACTION: Rarely.
HABIT: Upright
SIZE: 24" tall and wide.
LEAVES: 1 1/2–2" long, pointed, oval, green or purple.
FLOWERS: 1/2" long, white to lavender and appear throughout summer.
TEXTURE: Medium.
CULTURE: Full sun. Prefers rich, well drained soils.
LANDSCAPE/ GARDEN VALUE: Purple and ruffle leaf varieties are great for use in annual borders and beds, herb gardens. Good for containers.
HARDINESS: Not frost tolerant.
NATIVE HABITAT: India.
SPECIAL CHARACTERISTICS: Leaves repel insects. Used primarily in Mediterranean cuisine, most commonly used with tomatoes and for making pesto.

HERBS

Pimpinalla anisum
ANISE

DEER ATTRACTION: Rarely.
HABIT: Spreading.
SIZE: 24" tall, spreads 36" or more.
LEAVES: 4–6" long, green, deeply notched and aromatic.
FLOWERS: 3–4" heavy clusters of small yellowish-white flowers.
TEXTURE: Fine.
CULTURE: Full sun. Adapts to most any well drained soil. Tolerates hot, dry conditions.
LANDSCAPE/ GARDEN VALUE: Little or no ornamental value. Use in herb gardens.
HARDINESS: Not frost tolerant.
NATIVE HABITAT: Greece to Egypt.
SPECIAL CHARACTERISTICS: Leaves are used for flavoring foods. Seeds are used in curries and in Mediterranean and Chinese cuisine. Oil extract kills insects. Medicinal uses include treatment of indigestion, flatulence, coughs, and colic.

Ruta graveolens
RUE

DEER ATTRACTION: Rarely.
HABIT: Upright and shrubby.
SIZE: 36" tall, 24" wide.
LEAVES: Evergreen, 4–6" long, twice-compound, fragrant and green.
FLOWERS: 1/2" wide, yellow, and appear in July.
TEXTURE: Fine.
CULTURE: Full sun. Adapts to almost any well drained soil.
LANDSCAPE/ GARDEN VALUE: Use as a small shrub. Herb gardens.
HARDINESS: Zone 4.
NATIVE HABITAT: Southern Europe.
SPECIAL CHARACTERISTICS: Medicinal uses include the treatment of strains, sprains, eyestrain, headaches, heart palpitations, indigestion, parasitic worms, insect and snake bites, menstruation, rheumatic and other pains.

HERBS

Salvia officinalis
SAGE

DEER ATTRACTION: Rarely.
HABIT: Upright.
SIZE: 12–24" tall.
LEAVES: 2" long, oval, wrinkled, and covered with a white fuzz, very aromatic. Most common is green but red, golden, and multicolored varieties are available.
FLOWERS: 3/4" long, purplish-blue spikes appear in June through September. White and red flowering varieties are available.
TEXTURE: Medium.
CULTURE: Full sun. Any well drained soil.
LANDSCAPE/ GARDEN VALUE: Herb gardens, and containers. Varieties with red, golden, and multicolored leaves work well in annual and mixed flower beds as do white and red flowering varieties.
HARDINESS: Zone 3.
NATIVE HABITAT: Mediterranean area.
SPECIAL CHARACTERISTICS: In addition to their ornamental uses, Sage leaves are widely used with cooking pork and poultry and are believed to stimulate digestion. Also known as a healing herb, medicinal uses include treating sore throats, colds, indigestion, hot flashes, and pain. Sage tea is often used as a mouthwash.

Satureja montana
SAVORY

DEER ATTRACTION: Rarely.
HABIT: Upright.
SIZE: 12–16" tall and wide.
LEAVES: 1 1/2" long and narrow, green and aromatic.
FLOWERS: Inconspicuous, tiny purplish-pink flowers appear in summer.
TEXTURE: Fine.
CULTURE: Full sun. Any well drained soil.
LANDSCAPE/ GARDEN VALUE: Mainly herb gardens and containers.
HARDINESS: Zone 5.
NATIVE HABITAT: Europe.
SPECIAL CHARACTERISTICS: Leaves are used as flavoring with vegetables, legumes, and meats such as salami.

Acknowledgements

Many thanks to those gardeners who have sought my advice on this subject and encouraged my research into this important horticultural area. Further thanks go to Fred Hicks and the entire Hicks Nurseries Inc. staff, past and present, for their inspiration and encouragement through the years.

Selected References

Drzewucki Jr., Vincent. 1998 *Gardening In Deer Country-For the Home and Garden.* Brick Tower Press

Curtis, P.D, and M.E.Richmond. 1994. *Reducing Deer Damage to Home Gardens and Landscape Plantings.* Department of Natural Resources, Cornell University, Ithaca, New York 14853.

Jescavage-Bernard, Karen. 1991. *Gardening In Deer Country, Some Ornamental Plants for Eastern Gardens.* Karen Jescavage-Bernard, 529 E. Quaker Bridge Road, Croton-on-the-Hudson, NY 10529.

Sheets, Kathy. 1995. *Oh Deer! How to keep your treasured plants from becoming the main course, Fine Gardening* November/December 1995 No. 46. The Taunton Press, Inc., Newtown, CT 06470-5506.

Ag Information Services—News and Publications. Penn State College of Agricultural Sciences. 106 Ag. Adm., University Park, PA 16802-2602

Cornell Cooperative Extension, Cornell University, Ithaca, NY 14853.

For information in your area contact your state Department of Natural Resources and Environment, Fish, Game and Wildlife or State Cooperative Extension Service.

For Plants and Repellents (including Milorganite)

Hicks Nurseries Inc.
P.O. Box 648
100 Jericho Tpke.
Westbury, NY 11590
(516) 334-0066

INDEX

Latin names appear by plant group starting on page 39. If a Latin name appears below, the common name is the Latin name.

C

D

E, F

O

P

R

S

NOTES:

BRICK TOWER PRESS

MAIL ORDER AND GENERAL INFORMATION
Many of our titles are carried by your local book store or gift and museum shop. If they do not already carry our line please ask them to write us for information.

If you are unable to purchase our titles from your local shop, call or write to us. Our titles are available through mail order. Just send us a check or money order for $9.95 per title with $1.50 postage (shipping is free with 3 or more assorted copies) to the address below or call us Monday through Friday, 9 AM to 5PM, EST. We accept Visa, Mastercard, and American Express cards.

For sales, editorial information, subsidiary rights information or a catalog, please write or phone or e-mail to
Brick Tower Press
1230 Park Avenue
New York, NY 10128, US
Sales: 1-800-68-BRICK
Tel: 212-427-7139 Fax: 212-860-8852
www.BrickTowerPress.com
email: bricktower@aol.com.

For Canadian sales please contact our distributor,
Vanwell Publishing Ltd.
1 Northrup Crescent, Box 2131
St. Catharines, ON L2R 7S2
Tel: 905-937-3100

For sales in the UK and Europe please contact our distributor,
Gazelle Book Services
Falcon House, Queens Square
Lancaster, LA1 1RN, UK
Tel: (01524) 68765 Fax: (01524) 63232
email: gazelle4go@aol.com.

For Australian and New Zealand sales please contact
INT Press Distribution Pyt. Ltd.
386 Mt. Alexander Road
Ascot Vale, VIC 3032, Australia
Tel: 61-3-9326 2416 Fax: 61-3-9326 2413
email: sales@intpress.com.au.

Traditional Country Life Recipe Series
Financial Guides
Biography
Maritime Nonfiction
Military
Historical Fiction
Self-Development
Gardening